MW00425290

4/23

STRAND PRICE
$5.00

FROM
BRIGHTON BEACH
TO
MADISON AVENUE

TESTIMONIALS FOR DAVID C. WIENER

I've never known a successful person who didn't have a good accountant. David is to a good accountant what a Lamborghini is to your neighbor's SUV. Buying this book is like holding a Lamborghini ignition key in your hand. Reading the book is the best step you can take to creating the most value for your company. David's advice is golden. Trust me. I trusted him, and that was one of the Biggest Ideas I've had.

—Donny Deutsch, chairman, Deutsch Inc.

David is a unicorn. His unerring eye for detail, his insistence on financial best practices, and his total intolerance for laziness and stupidity make him one of my favorite people. His advice is invaluable to business owners, CEOs, and entrepreneurs in the marketing-services space. The best move you can make is to get David's accounting advice. The next best thing is to read his book, and if you can manage it, I recommend you do both.

—Marina Maher, CEO, Marina Maher Communications

David Wiener is the General Patton of dealmakers. When he's on your side, your opponents shiver in their boots and you win the war. David mows them down with his no-nonsense approach, a mix of street smarts and sound strategy. Read this book and learn how to win.

—Richard Kirshenbaum, CEO, Swat Advertising; author, *Rouge*

David is known as the "money guy": smart, diligent, and ethical. He is kind, generous and funny too, the best type of friend to have.

—Adelaide Horton, cofounder, Horton-Maroun Studio

My grandfather is the most amazing role model for me. Most people view him as stubborn, obnoxiously funny, so very smart, and an extremely successful businessman. That is all true, but I am lucky to see a side of my grandpa that no one else can find. He is soft and kind, lovable and loyal, and spoils me like crazy. I have of course added Papa's book to my summer reading list!

—Lexi Samuels, oldest granddaughter

David is an insightful businessman, tenacious negotiator, and a great advocate for his clients. He presents information with radical simplicity, no BS, and always a gentle (or not so gentle) dose of levity.

—David Demuth, CEO, Doner

David is one of the most honorable people I have worked with over my career. He negotiates hard but fair. Once he gives his word, you can take it to the bank.

—Jay Weinstein, partner, EisnerAmper

It's no secret that the advertising business is full of prima donnas, artistes, and egos the size of Trump Tower. What's amazing is that David has been able to herd, manage, persuade, and make deals with pretty much all of them. I hope he does an audio version of the book. There'll be a lot of yelling.

—Chuck Porter, chairman, Crispin Porter + Bogusky

David Wiener is a force of nature. He is sharp as a tack and someone who advocates feverishly for his clients. David always follows through with exactly what he said he will do. He therefore has a healthy degree of impatience for those who don't operate the same way. For those who do, David provides a master class in mergers and acquisitions involving the marketing communications industry. It's a class that any entrepreneur in the business should take.

—Brad J. Schwartzberg and Michael C. Lasky,
partners, Davis & Gilbert LLP

Mercury was a small shop with one office when we met David Wiener. His able guidance and deep Rolodex were key to our initial sale, and his continued strategic counsel helped us grow the company to eighteen offices. We could not have done that without the unique financial structure David helped create.

—Kieran Mahoney, managing partner, Mercury

David isn't a person; he's a force of nature. For decades, he did most if not all of the important deals in the advertising/marketing business. If that sounds like he's too serious for fun, he's not. He also has one of the nuttiest senses of humor of all time!

—Martin Puris, CEO, Puris & Partners

David Wiener has been counselor to many of the most significant entrepreneurs of the advertising industry for decades. His wisdom on business and in life is a treasure and an invaluable part of the story of 72andSunny.

—Matt Jarvis, CEO, 72andSunny

To the smartest, toughest, nicest, and funniest negotiator, counselor, and friend a guy could have. May this be a very happy and healthy milestone.

—Bruce Miller, president, Suissa Miller Advertising

As someone who can't always handle the truth, I have really treasured the advice David has given me over the years. He is forthright, funny, globally knowledgeable, and dammit, always right. I'm sure there are great lessons to be learned herein, and you won't have to pay as much as I did to learn them.

—Jeff Goodby, cochair, Goodby, Silverstein & Partners

Over a number of years, I have been privileged to work with David as his counsel and as counsel to a number of shared clients. David's business sense and knowledge are unique and extensive, and I have personally witnessed his ability to find hidden value for his clients. He is unique in many ways—including his ability to get deals done and in his facile and (at times) nuanced approach to clients and adversaries. David is extremely knowledgeable regarding the marketing services industry and has deep contacts with most of the major players. He is a significant figure in marketing service agency M&A, and I have been extremely fortunate to learn the business intricacies of these transactions from someone as gifted as David. In particular, I always consider myself to be very fortunate to be sitting on the same side of the table as David!

—Jeffrey M. Davis, Moses & Singer

It's not an easy task living with David. He keeps me on my toes constantly. He wants things his way and he works hard to get it. He is brilliant, humorous, exacting, and meticulous. He knows everything; the funny thing is, he really does! He is generous, charitable, and if he loves you he will go to the end of the earth for you. He makes me feel loved and special, and I laugh every day. In our home there is "Shalom Bayit." Over these past 50 years, I have learned so much from him. How can I thank you, David, for giving me a life that people only dream of, filled with laughter and love? Now that the process of writing this book is over, are you going to start nagging to clean out the closets and cabinets?

—(Mrs.) Sheila Wiener

David is an extraordinary individual, highly intelligent, very focused, and able to get transactions completed on a mutually beneficial basis. David has been an important factor to the success of MDC Partners' numerous iconic acquisitions of leading-edge agencies that have helped to contribute to MDC's reputation as a thought leader and the place where great talent lives.

—Miles Nadal, former CEO, MDC Partners

We interviewed many merger and acquisition firms. David was by far the most insightful and realistic. We loved his no-nonsense style, and within minutes we knew he was the one. He overdelivered!

—Madeline DeVries, chairman of the board, DeVries Public Relations

David was this sweet little yeshiva boychik who negotiated with as filthy a mouth and clarity of purpose as I could imagine. We did the deal and he invited me to go to a Friars Club roast with Sheila and my wife. And I hired him to do some work for Grey.

—Steven G. Felsher, former vice chairman and CFO, Grey Global Group Inc.

FROM BRIGHTON BEACH

TO MADISON AVENUE

THE REAL BUSINESS OF ADVERTISING

DAVID C. WIENER

Radius Book Group
New York

Distributed by Radius Book Group
A Division of Diversion Publishing Corp.
443 Park Avenue South, Suite 1004
New York, NY 10016
www.RadiusBookGroup.com

Copyright © 2018 by David C. Wiener

All rights reserved, including the right to reproduce this book or portions thereof in any form whatsoever. No part of this publication may be reproduced or transmitted in any form or by any means, electronic or mechanical, including photocopying, recording, or any other information storage and retrieval, without the written permission of the author.

For more information, email info@diversionbooks.com.

First edition: August 2018
Hardcover ISBN: 978-1-63576-571-7
eBook ISBN: 978-1-63576-572-4

Manufactured in the United States of America

10 9 8 7 6 5 4 3 2 1

Cover design by Erin New
Interior design and production by Scribe Inc.

Radius Book Group and the Radius Book Group colophon are registered trademarks of Radius Book Group, a Division of Diversion Publishing Corp.

This book is dedicated to my wonderful wife and life partner, Sheila, who has put up with my passion for work, for taking risks, and for living with my profession each and every day that we've been together for more than fifty years.

It is also dedicated to my three children, who, I hope, understand that many of the hours at my desk, days away from home, and time spent working and reading were for their benefit and future.

The book is also dedicated to my late dear friend, mentor, client, and hero, Jay Chiat, who had faith in me, constantly drove me by reminding me that "good enough is not enough," and allowed me to share a time with him somewhat similar to *Camelot*.

Finally, I hope this book will be a tome to my grandchildren—Alexis, Samantha, and Max—to work hard, to believe in themselves, to remember me with a smile, and to give them a little peek into what their Papa did with much of his life and how we became a family that enjoyed many laughs, memories, and a sense of joy and security.

CONTENTS

ACKNOWLEDGMENTS

So many people helped shape my life and career and motivated me to write this book that I cannot thank them all.

Among those who influenced me greatly early in my career were Bentley Paykin, the Ostrowitz brothers, Seymour Graham, Sydney Hyman, Seymour Goldstein, Jay Chiat, and Donny Deutsch.

I have been blessed with great clients, many of whom have become great friends: Mike Kooper, Jeff Weiss, Fred Goldberg, and Richard Kirshenbaum, to name a few.

I have learned a great deal from industry colleagues—Fred Meyer, Dale Adams, Ed Meyer, Tim Andree, Tom Harrison, Miles Nadal, Jeff Davis, Brad Schwartzberg, and Michael Lasky.

I could not have achieved much of what I have done without my business colleagues and partners over the years, including Harold Goldman; Carey Gertler; Warren Suna; Bruce Baron; my late sister, Ruth Wiener; the late Gil Shelton; and Karen Sellers.

Jeff Weiss and Michael Friedman encouraged me and helped me put the team together to get the idea of a book down on paper—or at least in electronic ink.

Thanks to Warren Strugatch, my collaborator in writing this book, who reluctantly put up with my constant editing and my desire to be edgy—his efforts to write in my voice are appreciated.

Thanks to my publisher Scott Waxman, editor Mark Fretz, and the superb team at Radius Book Group for their help getting the book written, edited, designed, and printed.

I cannot fully express the huge sense of gratitude and respect I have for my late parents, Ben and Pearl Wiener, for their nurturing, understanding, and patience and the lessons they taught me during difficult times. I thank them for all they've done every day and hope Sheila and I were able to make life a little less difficult for them.

So many people helped shape my life and career that if I were to include all their names, it would make *War and Peace* seem like a short story. However, I would like to name a few. To those whose names I unintentionally omitted, I apologize and thank you now for the experiences and the opportunities.

Alvin Achenbaum	Kirill Goncharenko	Miles Nadal
Dale Adams	Jeff Goodby	Terry Nelson
John Adams	Barry Gosin	Jane Newman
Reis Alfond	Jay Gould*	Wes Nichols
Scott Allison	Jeff Grabel	Fabian Nunez
Ralph Ammirati	Seymour Graham*	Sean Orr
Tim Andree	Donna Granato	Milton Ostrowitz*
Tony Angotti	Nancy Granetz	Sidney Ostrowitz*
Jack Avrett*	Dan Gregory	David Paine
Aubrey Balkind	Carl Grossman*	Phil Palazzo
Spencer Baretz	Gerry Grossman*	Ben Paykin*
James Bargon	Steve Groth	Len Pearlstein
Bruce Baron	Henry Halpern*	Ric Peralta
Gene Beard	Bill Hamilton	Bob Perkins
David Bell	Bob Hanley	Leo Permutico
Andy Berlin	Andy Hardie-Brown	Brock Pernice
John Bernbach	Elizabeth Harrison	Chuck Phillips
Harry Bernstein	Tom Harrison	Clint Pierce
Michael Birkin	Michael Hart	Faith Popcorn
Mike Blatter	John Hayes	Chuck Porter
Bob Bloom	Barrie Hedge	Peter Post
Jeff Bogursky	Jeff Hicks	Jennifer Prosek
Alex Bogusky	Jim Holbrook	John Puglisi
John Boiler	Dennis Holt	Martin Puris
Jon Bond	Tony Hopp	Jordan Rednor
Margi Booth	Rob Horler	Arlene Reiser
Jean Claude Boulet	Charlie Horsey	Phil Reiss*

Yuriy Boykiv	Adelaide Horton	Gary Reynolds
Rick Boyko	Doug Houston*	David Ross
Keith Bremer	Mike Hughes*	Michael Roth
Keith Bright	Sydney Hyman*	Peter Rothenberg*
Matt Bryant	Victor Imbimbo	Herb Rowland*
John Butler	Bob Ingram	Lew Rubin
Nick Camera	Jan Jacobs	Bill Russell
Tom Carroll	Matt Jarvis	Andrew Sacks
Alex Chernoff	Michael Jeary	Marian Salzman
Jay Chiat*	Bob Jeffrey	Buz Sawyer
Loretta Chiat Mufson	Tibor Kalman*	Linda Sawyer
Harry Clark	Nina Kaminer	Bob Schmidt
Lee Clow	Mark Kaminsky	Yehochai (Joe) Schneider
Morgan Clyne*	Bob Kantor	Gerald Schwartz
Joey Cohen	Linus Karlsson	Brad Schwartzberg
Rob Colangelo	Scott Kauffman	Jim Scott
Glenn Cole	Allan Kay	Karen Sellers
Don Coleman	Paul Kelly	Jamie Seltzer
Marty Cooke	Richard Kirshenbaum	Lori Senecal
Jim Cotter	Dan Klores	Michael Sennott
Jim Cowperthwait	Mike Kooper	Mike Sheldon
Tom Cox	Ray Kotcher	Gil Shelton*
Bruce Crawford	Philippe Krakowsky	Rob Shepardson
Brian Curran	Peter Krivkovich	Brett Shevack
Alfonse D'Amato	Howard Kroplick	Mike Shine
Elaine Dannheisser*	Mike Kubin	Steve Shlansky
Steve Dapper	Bob Kuperman	Lara Shriftman
Frank Darcy	Rick Kurnit	Allan Siegel
Clyde Davis	Aaron Kwittken	Tony Signore
Jeff Davis	Bob Laidman	Michael Silberberg*
Guy Day*	Trey Laird	Jon Silvan
Rob DeFlorio	Chris Lange	Rich Silverstein
Jerry Della Femina	Joe LaRosa	Lew Simon*

Dave DeMuth	Mike Lasky	Cliff Sloan
Donny Deutsch	David Lehv	Roger Slotkin
Madeline DeVries	Grace Leong	Marvin Sloves
Harris Diamond	Kal Liebowitz	Jeff Snyder
Rob Dickson	Maureen Lippe	Erik Sollenberg
Mike Ditzian*	Howard Liszt	Ed Spiro
David Doft	Bob Livingston	Sharon Stanley
Paul Donaher	Frank Lowe	Greg Stern
John Doolittle	Dan Lufkin	Lenny Stern
John Dooner	Lindsay Lustberg	Michael Stone
Henry Dosch	Lee Lynch	Greg Strimple
Mark Dowley	Jon Lyon	David Suissa
Jean Marie Dru	Ann Maher	Warren Suna
Terry Dry	Marina Maher	Peter Swain
Mike DuHaime	Kieran Mahoney	Dick Tarlow
Ari Emanuel	Mary-Jean Malone Koster	Tom Thomas
Saul Erdman*	Fred Mann	Bill Tragos
Ed Eskandarian	Tom Marino	John Vassallo
Ken Eudy	Michael Mark	Tony Wainwright
Pat Fallon*	Jim Marlis	Peter Walker
Steve Felsher	Greg Marsh	Saul Waring*
George Fertitta	Bob Marston	Tom Watson
Ron Fierman	Ira Matathia	Chris Weil
Andy Fletcher	Ed McCabe	Jay Weinstein
Cliff Freeman	David McCall*	Davis Weinstock
Michael Friedman	Jim McCann	Larry Weintraub
Sol Friedman	Tom McElligott	Randy Weisenburger
Frank Gehry	Ed Meyer	Jeff Weiss
Phil Geier	Fred Meyer	Ruth Wiener*
Jerry Germain	Bruce Miller	Paul Wilmot
Carey Gertler	Floyd Miller	Jason Winocour
Joe Gilbride	Scott Miller	Bob Wolf
Frank Ginsberg	Elyse Mitchell	Larry Wolff

Rick Glosman	Robert Morvillo*	John Wren
Fred Goldberg	Jarrod Moses	Jordan Zimmerman
Harold Goldman	Sheldon Mufson*	Jerry Zuckerman
Gary Goldsmith	Donna Murphy	Karen Zuckerman
Seymour Goldstein*	Bill Murray	Sergio Zyman

* Deceased.

DCW
March 30, 2018

CHAPTER 1

TRADE MISSION TO MOSCOW

It was evening in Moscow, October 1989. Jay Chiat and I had just gone through Kremlin security and were seated at a table in a large, ornate conference room. I was almost hyperventilating. I leaned over to Jay and whispered, "Do you know what we're doing here? What's the likelihood we're going to actually pull this trade deal off?"

"I have no freaking idea," Jay said. "But you know what? Neither do those jerks in the conference room. They're empty suits. We're winging it, David. Let's just go with the flow. And relax."

He asked where the men's room was, and we both excused ourselves and headed there; it bought me time to compose myself.

Morton Jay Chiat, universally known as Jay, was my first advertising agency client, a mentor in business and life, and at that moment, my globe-trotting partner in our ill-fated trading company, Torg. Jay, of course, was one of the twentieth century's pre-eminent advertising executives, the chairman and chief executive of the legendary Chiat/Day. Bronx born, Jersey raised, and California cool, he is remembered for his role in creating the iconic "1984" ad for Apple

Russian vodka, and Russia itself, held an outward glamour for me until I experienced the country's seediness and shortages firsthand.

Computer that aired during Super Bowl XVIII, plus dozens of other remarkable, groundbreaking ads.

Everybody in the ad business from the seventies through the nineties remembers him fondly, even those he drove crazy, which was most of them. He was one of the most visionary, contradictory, confounding, funny, and ultimately lovable men in the business.

Torg was Jay's brainchild—make that brain fart. I helped him launch it, helped finance it by matching his half-million-dollar investment, and handled the books and most of the travel and negotiations. The Soviet agricultural trade board bought a minority stake, and we took on a pair of Russian immigrants as partners. We thought they were wily, but they turned out to be whack jobs.

Our plan was to swap Soviet commodities for US-manufactured products and make a few bucks in the process.

Clearly Jay and I were out of our element. Jay had never imported or exported anything in his life and knew nothing about trade finance. I knew a little bit—my clients often bartered one commodity for another—but I was no expert. And together we spoke maybe six words of Russian.

But Jay didn't allow any of these things to stand in our way. Torg was kind of a lark for Jay, a side project he undertook more to experience new challenges than to make tons of money. He loved facing down risk, loved living on the edge. His ex-partner, Guy Day, called him a born gambler. Whatever he did, he did with intensity. His passion attracted employees, investors, partners, and clients. He had more energy and vision than anyone I've ever met. Even running a juggernaut of an ad agency and spouting dozens of contradictory messages daily failed to absorb the entirety of his energy.

Jay was a brilliant, albeit inconsistent, businessman. We came into each other's lives in a roundabout way. I had met his sister at a party in New York. She was married to a client of mine. After she and I talked a while, she noticed we were both impatient, demanding, blunt, thick skinned, and smart and felt we were well matched, so she insisted I call him.

We met, we clicked, and he soon began assigning me various internal projects. Before long, he placed me on his board. He eventually asked me to become his full-time CFO, but I wasn't about to give up my accounting practice, so I turned him down.

Jay could also be perverse as hell. Once he draped his arm around my shoulder and counseled me to double my fees across the board.

"David," Jay said, "you look like crap. Take my advice and double your rates. Your clients will think you're worth more to them."

Even though he seemed serious, I simply replied, "I'll think about it."

But Jay was not satisfied; he said that if by raising my rates I lost half my business, I'd still make the same amount of money, and then I'd have some time away from work.

He sent someone to my office for my Rolodex, a box of stationery with my letterhead, and envelopes. He had a copywriter—Jamie Seltzer—compose a letter to all my clients that said my fees would double and that, sure, there were cheaper accountants, but what were you going to do with that extra money—have Earl Scheib paint your car?

After the letters had been prepared, he told me we should mail them and then go to lunch. I hesitated, but Jay would not hear of it. And so, on the corner of Fifth Avenue and Sixteenth Street, there was a mailbox with my letters in it—and my vomit all over the ground near it.

Note that I only lost one client as a result of the increase, and though I did not reduce my workload, I did make more money and set the stage for a premium-priced practice.

After I increased my prices, Jay ducked my calls for weeks—we had typically talked almost every day. When I finally reached him at home late at night, I asked him why he wasn't returning my calls.

"You raised your rates," Jay replied. "I can't afford you anymore."

He fired me more times than I can remember. But he always rehired me without comment, usually immediately, and certainly whenever a new project needed someone with a head for numbers, financial savvy, and maybe a bit of caution to counter his impulsivity. Once he fired me during a meeting, met me in the men's room, and rehired me before he flushed the toilet.

Despite his capriciousness, when my dad took ill, Jay asked if I was able to pay for all his medical bills. I said I'd manage, but Jay being Jay wrote me a check for $1 million and told me to use it as needed and to pay him back when I could.

The idea behind Torg was promising. The Soviet Union was great with propaganda, not so great with providing necessities to its citizens. They clearly needed US consumer goods and industrial equipment and other products, even if they officially denied it. Both countries outlawed the exchange of money for goods and services with the other. The roots of the disagreement went back to the aftermath of World War II, when the US applied trade sanctions to Russia and its allies as economic pressure.

Still, the Soviet Union comprised one of the world's biggest markets. Multinationals like Pepsi-Cola and Philip Morris yearned to do business there. Jay saw the opportunity and jumped right in. When Jay first proposed the trading company to me, I immediately thought of the challenges we'd face given the icy relations between the two governments. I thought of using countertrade as a work-around. A variation on barter, it had become popular in states whose currencies were not recognized outside their own borders. I tried to provide him with a brief introduction to it, but Jay was not sitting still for a finance lecture, from me or anyone else.

"Great, great," he said. "That's your thing, David. I'm with you on it."

Thanks in part to his vast network, we had lined up dozens of companies ready to sell to the USSR. Our aces in the hole were General Foods and Philip Morris, which agreed to supply us with manufactured products to exchange.

A Russian once told me that the word *torg* literally means "trade" but also means "haggling"—which is how you get what you want in Russia. Our negotiating partners, the four Russian agricultural officials, certainly understood that practice. When we first met, they gave us a directory the size of a Manhattan phone book. It was filled with hundreds of products they were prepared to swap in exchange for our services. One of these products was pigs' feet, to be processed and made into collagen. Collagen is used in making gelatin and cosmetic products and so has a defined market value in the US—provided, of course, one could consistently deliver quality product.

That was a big "if."

After spending a few days in Moscow, which included a little sight-seeing with Lev, one of our partners, Jay and I realized that we could not take the Soviets' official supplier list at face value. The list was primarily wishful thinking. In Russia, we learned, what you couldn't see and touch didn't exist. The country was plagued by shortages. There was no toilet paper in the restrooms. There was no soap in hotel showers, and if there was, it was the size of a nickel. If water ran in the sink, consider yourself lucky.

At the market, the produce was spotted or rotting. You'd buy several bags of apples and potatoes and slice away the inedible parts to produce maybe one apple's worth or one potato's worth of produce. You'd order beer in a restaurant or bar, and half the time they'd say they were out of it. They always had vodka, though—like Newcastle running out of coal, it'll never happen. Lev let us know that if we really wanted something—really, really wanted it—then maybe we should do what we did in America. We nodded but didn't pick up on his meaning. The second time he said it, we quickly understood: money talks, and here it spoke Russian. But it was illegal for Soviet citizens to own US dollars, so we turned to barter. You'd be amazed what a carton of Marlboro cigarettes could buy in Moscow. We finally had our toilet paper, soap, and other necessities.

The Soviets definitely wanted what we had to sell, which included everything from cigarettes and detergents to instant coffee and aspirin, plus all sorts of industrial and consumer commodities. How the Soviets would pay for any of it, however, was a conversation killer. To keep the talks alive, we looked more closely at their official list of agricultural and consumer products.

Our market forays had not whetted our appetite for Soviet agricultural products. However, it was becoming clear some of these products were better than others. The best was barely edible.

Potatoes from Siberia were a shaky proposition, but wines from Georgia? Georgia was a breadbasket of the Soviet Union. What grew there was prized in kitchens from one end of the empire to the other. Surely Georgian wines were at least drinkable.

After a few days of haggling—given our trade name, our hosts must have expected this—we came to terms on a deal. We agreed to ship them instant coffee and some other products in return for wine from Georgia and chocolate from a plant near Moscow. It was a small deal, but at least it offered a starting point. We figured the chocolate would handle the shipping well, and the wine would survive the overseas voyage better than fruit.

Our hosts asked us to send over some Montblanc pens and a few cases of Dom Pérignon so we might celebrate our deal in style the following day in the Soviet embassy in Washington, DC. We complied. At the signing, there was no evidence of either Dom Pérignon or Montblanc. The officials looked us dead in the eyes and declared the pens and booze had mysteriously disappeared. They substituted them with Soviet-made ballpoint pens and Soviet champagne. I used my own pen to sign and passed on the bubbly. As I recall, so did Jay. This may have been the most expensive drink we never had.

About a month later, we received our shipment of Georgian wines freshly delivered on an Aeroflot flight. We stored them in the only space available at my office: a conference room. When we opened the cartons the next day, every last bottle had popped its cork. The room reeked of fermented grape juice.

As for the chocolate, I took home a few cartons. They were beautifully wrapped in foil with depictions of stacking dolls. But one bite was more than enough; I spat it out. So did my wife, Sheila. *Awful* was too nice a word. We had sampled the chocolate during the trip; it had tasted much better in Russia. Selling it was going to be impossible. Sheila and I donated several boxes to a homeless shelter some miles away from our house. A week later, when we returned with several more boxes, we were told thanks but no thanks: the homeless people had refused to eat it. Eventually we threw the cartons away.

The miserable chocolate and the exploding wine were our initial experiences with "easy" products in the Soviet Union, and they failed to be suitable, saleable, or tradeable. Jay and I shared Eastern European ancestry, and I think we both understood the life experiences of our kin a little better after our travels. What struck us both were the deprivations of daily life and the constant presence of incompetence and corruption. The experience gave both of us, I think, a renewed appreciation of the free market. Capitalism has its shortcomings, but there is nothing like spending a week in the Soviet Union to make you appreciate the wisdom of keeping private enterprise out of government hands.

Also, I came of age during a time when America feared the USSR and its perceived might more than anything else in the world. To visit Russia and see how people lived was to experience a country that couldn't keep toilet paper in its bathrooms or put food on its tables. The average citizen couldn't get through the day without paying a bribe. If a country could not even keep toilet paper in its bathrooms or put food on its tables—in other words, provide for its citizens the basic necessities—what threat could it have posed to us?

Jay and I closed Torg soon after that. As global traders, we were not empire builders. Jay, however, continued to bring me into one remarkable agency project after another. Through him I took part in some of the most exciting developments in advertising in the eighties and nineties, experienced his visionary management style firsthand, and met a number of people who would play vital roles in my career.

CHAPTER 2

BRIGHTON BEACH

I was the first child born to Benjamin and Pearl Wiener of Brighton Beach, Brooklyn. I was the first grandson of Nathan and Rose Jacowitz, Rumanian immigrants, on my mother's side, and the third to Abraham and Ida Wiener, on my father's side. From a very young age, I was aware that my family held very high expectations for me, and I was determined to live up to them—in my own way.

We lived in a two-bedroom walk-up apartment on Brighton Beach Avenue and the corner of Twelfth Street, above a kosher butcher, a drug store, and a barbershop. I shared a bedroom with my younger sister, Ruth, until I was in high school. Then my grandfather Nathan, whom I called Zaydeh (Yiddish for "Grandfather"), moved in, and Ruth took the fold-out couch in the living room. There was a lot of love in our apartment, but not a lot of space.

Zaydeh taught me two expressions that Sheila and I still use to this day. My family only had one bathroom in that walk-up for the five people living in it. The bathroom was rarely unoccupied, so Zaydeh would knock on the door and say, "When you go out, I go in." Sheila and I have eight bathrooms in our home, but we still joke about it at home and use his phrase when we are in a hotel room. The second expression is always in use and is incredibly practical. If he wore a pair of pants one day and they were clean enough to wear another day, he called them "clean dirty," but if they were muddy or were worn several times already, he called them "dirty dirty." Think about it!

I started yeshiva—Jewish religious schooling—at age five, and some of my earliest memories are of that school. There I met about twenty-four other boys, three of whom were also named David. There were no girls; yeshiva instruction is sex segregated. For eight years, I saw these same boys almost every day.

If you've seen *Brighton Beach Memoirs*, the movie or stage play by Neil Simon, you would recognize scenes from my Brooklyn boyhood—the same if you've heard Neil Diamond's moving lyrics to "Brooklyn Roads" or some of Alan King's comedy monologues. Adjacent to Coney Island but spared its cheesy boardwalk attractions, Brighton Beach was a little more isolated, a little more backwater. The world came to Coney Island and mostly left Brighton Beach alone.

Brighton Beach was a little like the shtetls—insular Jewish communities in Eastern Europe—from which my grandparents had emigrated. It was predominantly an insulated, heavily Jewish lower-middle-class neighborhood. Almost everyone I knew until I went to high school was Jewish. Most of my family—aunts, uncles, and cousins—lived within a four- or five-block radius. When I walked down the street, I always saw people I knew, friends or family members. All the family who lived in the area were from my mother's side; my father had a very small family. I idolized my uncle Paul, who in retrospect was something of a rebel—he was educated, lived outside the local neighborhood, drove a luxury car, and owned a home, which was very different from how the rest of the family lived.

Uncle Paul was preoccupied by one thing, and what it was I could not have yet named at that early age. By the time I could, I was preoccupied by it too. He was a wild card, the closest thing to a cowboy my family had. His sense of freedom—maybe it was his *yearning* for freedom—inspired me. He died very young. I named my son after him.

When I walked down my block, even if I didn't see family or friends, you can believe they saw me: the walls had ears—and eyes. When I would go out to play, my parents would learn of my behavior—especially misbehavior—long before I got back. They would be ready for me.

I mostly didn't have time for playing, though. My life growing up was all about yeshiva. I spent six days a week and twelve hours a day there. It started at 6:30 in the morning, and I would wake up at four so I wasn't late. Often when we got out, it was already dark. I usually went straight home and did homework until dinner. After dinner, more homework. My parents made sure I always had a space in the apartment to study. For years it was a bridge table, later a small desk.

The work, which was a combination of secular studies and Judaic instruction, came easily to me. I didn't particularly like it; I just did it. In school *A*s were expected, and *A*s were delivered. I did so well that my third-grade teacher skipped me to the fifth grade. She tried to skip me again the next year, but my mother said no. I imagine she understood I needed to develop social skills as well as academic ones and needed to fit in with my peer group. We never discussed it.

Yeshiva's workload and its relentless discipline instilled in me a strong work ethic that has enriched my life. When you put in twelve-hour workdays at age ten, continuing that at age thirty—or seventy, as I am today—comes naturally. To this day, I still wake up at four every morning to start my work.

Yeshiva ingrained in me the question-and-answer approach to solving problems that is the Jewish people's Talmudic legacy. How do I know that? When my step-grandmother took me to see *Fiddler on the Roof* on Broadway, I recognized the yeshiva sensibility behind Tevye's running commentary on life's puzzles, indignities, and absurdities. Joseph Stein clearly understood yeshiva life.

The education we received at yeshiva was a little like going to law school in short pants. We learned and memorized a long series of laws and rules. The challenge was discovering for ourselves the underlying logic. These rules existed to ensure that the Jewish people followed the path of righteousness. They also were intended to ensure our survival as a people.

Yeshiva, parochial as it was, also greatly prepared me for my further education. I not only learned how to learn but received the foundational education that serves me to this day. I mean this literally. High school and college presented very few major challenges for me. I had been thoroughly prepared by my teachers in yeshiva.

Despite my enthusiasm for it now, when I was in double-digit years, I began to rebel against that nose-to-the-grindstone ethos. I told my parents I wanted out of Sunday school. They accepted this, and finally I had a little time of my own. I began going outside more and exploring the neighborhood.

I had two cousins close to me in age, Steven and Ronald, and for much of my childhood, we ran around together. We rode bikes; played ring-a-levio, that marvelous New York City answer to hide-and-seek; and played softball and stickball. When it was my turn at bat, I always imagined myself as Mickey Mantle. Why Mick? He was number 7 on the Yankees, and seven is my lucky number, corresponding to my birthday: 7/27/1947. Most of the other kids in the neighborhood rooted for the Brooklyn Dodgers.

My Mickey Mantle hero worship didn't make me a better ballplayer, although I wasn't terrible. I enjoyed playing the game, and I enjoyed watching the pros. New York had three professional baseball teams in those years: the Yankees, the Dodgers, and the Giants. I remember seeing a few Dodgers games with my father at Ebbets Field. After the team moved in 1958, my father took me to Yankee Stadium a few times. I also followed football and the Giants. I saw my first live NFL game in my midtwenties, when a client with Jets season tickets invited me as his guest.

I did enjoy going to the movies. Usually accompanied by one or two of my cousins, I went to the Oceana Movie Theater, which was a block from our apartment. I remember seeing *Ben-Hur*, starring Charlton Heston, when it came out. The movie made a big impression on me and remains one of my favorites.

My other form of entertainment was reading. As much as I learned in yeshiva, it was reading that really opened the world to me. We had an almanac that I read like a novel, cover to cover. I couldn't put it down. One of my aunts had a set of *Encyclopædia Britannica*. When I was eleven, she let me borrow one book at a time. Before I was thirteen, I had read through the set, *A* to *Z*. I got razzed about it by my friends. When yeshiva boys tease you for reading too much, it's time to worry.

My family was lower middle class with very little disposable income. Years later, I realized we, like most of our neighbors, had a relatively narrow view of the world. For instance, a family who lived down the block told us they were moving to Bensonhurst in Brooklyn, and my mother cried bitter tears, sure she would never see them again. When my mother's sister and her family moved to the Midwest, it might as well have been a move to Siberia.

My mother was always quite ill. She had type 2 diabetes, high blood pressure, and myasthenia gravis, which left her weak and immobile. She had a laundry list of other health issues: arthritis, gallbladder problems, and a history of ministrokes. She was also very heavy, and that brought on additional problems. Sadly, just being alive was an ordeal for her. She died at age fifty-eight after five years of suffering from lymphoma.

Despite my mother's travails, she was incredibly loving and warm and lived her life with a sense of grace that endeared her to everyone who knew her. She was a kind, caring mother. Of course, all parents sooner or later have to discipline their children—spare the rod, spoil the child, as they say. Mom didn't punish us often, but once in a great while, after some infraction, there was a quick whack. On rare occasions, she would also dole out the silent treatment. Rare as this was, the withdrawal of her normal maternal warmth shook us to the core. I think she knew this, which is why she used it sparingly.

My dad was warm and loving too, just less inclined to show it. He had had a miserable childhood. At the age of ten or eleven, his mother sent him away to live in a residential camp in Upstate New York that entertainer Eddie Cantor founded for needy kids, allegedly since the camp could better treat his medical problems: he suffered from serious migraines. Growing up in dormitories meant he was never comfortable revealing his emotions. However, he was very loyal to his family. He put us first, ensuring we'd have a better life than he. He was a role model for me.

My father struggled all his life to make a buck, or rather make enough bucks. He sold drugs and drug store products for a pharmaceutical wholesaler, but his salary never seemed to be enough. I always remember him coming home at the end of the day, walking up the steps, slowly opening the front door, and entering, his sample case preceding him into the hallway. Years later, when I saw Arthur Miller's play *Death of a Salesman*, I thought immediately of my father. Miller was another Brooklyn boy; we graduated from the same high school.

My father drove Fords and Chevys. Many men in the neighborhood did not have cars, and I think he enjoyed the prestige of owning one despite their no-frills status. He was on the road most of the time, visiting customers in New Jersey or the Bronx. My first exposure to the business world came in a conversation with him where I asked why he didn't sell his wares to the drugstore right downstairs. He patiently explained that salesmen had territories—his was New Jersey and the Bronx, and another salesman had this one.

"But, Dad," I said, "we live in this building!"

"So?" he said. "It doesn't matter."

It seemed terribly unfair. But Dad didn't seem to care, so I got over it.

My father always worked hard. Even though he never put it into words, I knew he was working to give me and Ruth opportunities. One night, I overheard my parents arguing over money. I started to realize that even if you worked hard, you might not have enough money for necessities, let alone the extra things you might want to buy for yourself or those you loved. You needed a skill that would always be in demand.

That conversation was unusual; my parents rarely argued, it seemed to me, and besides, adults never talked about money within earshot of their children. If someone asked how you were doing, you'd say, "Oh, I'm comfortable." It always brought to my mind the image of someone resting in one of those easy chairs, where the back slides down and a footrest materializes. You put your feet up, maybe light up a cigar and smoke it. That's comfortable, right?

I was determined from an early age to become very, very comfortable. I was probably eight or nine when I promised myself that one day I'd be able to buy a Cadillac for my father and a mink coat for my mother. These were the standard unattainable status symbols of Brighton Beach, the visible proof that you'd achieved success in the world.

In my midtwenties, after a very financially successful year, I took my wife and my mother shopping and bought them both fur coats. But my father was a little different. His sense of pride would never allow him to accept the Caddy from me as a gift, so I told him that the dealership in New Jersey I used would sell him a car at a steep discount—in reality, I'd pay the difference of the "discount." The discount—my gift to him—was so huge that he immediately got on the phone and dialed his cronies, alerting them to this dealership that was practically giving Caddies away. I had to take him aside and tell him the discount was special to him only and nontransferrable. I don't know if he ever figured out what happened.

Like many Jewish families, we went every summer to the Catskill Mountains, where we stayed in a hotel for a week, crowded into one room. In our circles, no one flew to the Caribbean, motored up to the Berkshires, or rented a house in the Hamptons. That was for rich people. We went to the "Mountains." Once there, the major topic was food. We talked about food incessantly: how good it was, or not, and—especially—how much of it there was. Most hotels offered unlimited meal plans, and all week long we took advantage of it. We also enjoyed the recreational opportunities, the comedy shows, and the great outdoors.

For a couple of summers, we broke out of hotel mode and, along with my mother's sister or cousin and their families, rented a small *kuchalayn*—Yiddish for "cook it yourself"—in what was known as a bungalow colony: a collection of small bungalows that shared a campus with a lake or a pool, grass fields, laundry rooms, and a social hall, called the casino.

Whereas the hotels bragged about their facilities, their rooms, and their entertainment, the bungalow colonies were the opposite: simple and spare. If the Catskills had a motto, it would have been "Too much is not enough." The *kuchalayn* were the opposite. You cooked your own food; you made your own fun. We found we enjoyed cooking meals together more than bingeing on hotel food. We went on walks together, and I got to play softball and spend time with my cousins.

Other than anticipating the annual week or two in the mountains, in Brighton Beach in the fifties, people didn't aspire to very much. No one dreamed of, or planned for, getting a Manhattan apartment, buying a suburban house, or entering a licensed profession, unless it was teaching. No one made plans to travel overseas, obtain a graduate degree, or learn a foreign language.

When eighth grade was about to end, the principal called my parents and me in for a meeting. This was highly unusual, and I didn't know what to expect. My jaw dropped when he told us not only that I qualified for a full scholarship to attend an Orthodox yeshiva high school but that the school would also pay my parents a substantial monthly honorarium. This subsidy might startle parents today, in these times of astronomical tuition bills, but the offer reflected the age-old tradition of Eastern Europe, where the community supported those they perceived as young Jewish scholars. That tradition was transferred to the New World and continued in neighborhoods like Brighton Beach.

I considered the offer, but in the end, I decided the yeshiva education and accompanying lifestyle were too insular. I had begun to notice the girls who frequented the beach just across the street, who would not be my classmates if I were to attend a yeshiva high school. I was very aware that the public high school was co-ed. I was becoming more cognizant of the outside world and yearned to experience it. When I told my parents I would turn down the scholarship and attend public school, they didn't argue or challenge my decision. I realize today, though, that it must have been enormously frustrating to them; the money I turned down would have paid an awful lot of bills. But they graciously accepted my decision and never mentioned it again.

CHAPTER 3

ABRAHAM LINCOLN HIGH SCHOOL
AND BROOKLYN COLLEGE

I walked through the colossal front doors of Abraham Lincoln High School in the fall of 1960, entering a sea of adolescent faces. My class included more than three thousand students, very few of whom I knew. Lincoln's study hall was bigger than the entire yeshiva. I felt like a fish out of water.

I had chosen to attend public school because I wanted a more diverse and less insular culture, and at Lincoln I found it: along with us Jews, there were African Americans, Italians, Hispanics, and Asians. Still, diversity was a relative matter; Jews represented approximately 85 percent of the student body and nearly the entire faculty. At lunch the first day, I sat down at a cafeteria table with strangers of different races and ethnicities. Some of those strangers, happily, were female, something not possible at yeshiva. We all exchanged names, and I made my first non-Jewish friends—and realized that after you've had lunch with people a few times, they start to seem less different from you, and you start to seem less different from them.

In New York at that time (as well as now), you had a choice of high schools. You could enroll in your local district school or you could apply to magnet schools. Magnet schools tended to be specialized and competitive, meaning you had to pass their tests to register. Often there were different programs at each school, and each program had its own requirements and enrollment process. It wasn't simple.

When applying, I took tests for several magnet schools, including Brooklyn Tech and Bronx Science. Brooklyn Tech was composed mostly of boys who planned to become engineers. Neither characteristic appealed to me. Bronx Science was known for nurturing whip-smart students and actually enrolled girls. However, it was located in the Bronx, which would have kept me on the subways three hours a day. So that nixed Bronx Science. Lincoln was nearby on Ocean Parkway, so it won out over the others, and my public school education began.

Two of the big pop singers of yesteryear—Neil Diamond and Neil Sedaka—are linked by their first names, their Brooklyn upbringings, and, less famously, their connection to me. Neil Sedaka had graduated from Lincoln High School seven or eight years ahead of me, and the Sedakas were family friends. As for Neil Diamond, he also graduated from Lincoln ahead of me, behind Sedaka, and his parents owned the sundries store around the corner from our apartment. We bought our socks and underwear there.

At the time, doo-wop vocalizing was in vogue; small groups of boys would often harmonize their songs in the halls, stairways, or bathrooms of Lincoln. Our instructor started the semester with a mass musical audition. My "friends," the two singing Neils, played a little joke on me and told the instructor that I was the next great voice of our generation, so I was picked first for the audition. I had to go on stage and sing to test my voice, and I'm sure I tested the instructor—at least his patience. When I started to sing, my voice cracked—after all, I was only thirteen years old. The teacher asked me to try again, and once again, my voice cracked, as if on cue.

"Cut it out, David," the teacher said.

"I can't," I replied. "That's my voice."

Word spread—teenagers don't need much to start gossiping—and I became the kid who could make his voice crack on command. In the hallways, the students would joke, "Hey, David, you wanna sing at my sister's wedding?" or "Would you sing at my brother's bar mitzvah?" I turned down all offers.

The sixties was a turbulent period in New York City. In many schools, gangs were prevalent and the threat of violence was near constant. But this was not the case at Lincoln; there were no gangs, and I remember no violence. For the most part, we all got along.

As time went on, I made more friends and got involved in sports, particularly football. In the summers, I would hang out at the beach with my friends. We'd talk about girls and ways to start conversations with them—sometimes we even managed to actually talk to some. Occasionally conversations led to new discoveries. I was never a great swimmer, but I learned there were other things besides swimming you could do in the ocean.

I felt a bit less pressure at Lincoln to succeed academically. In many ways, my schoolwork was easier than at yeshiva. I was almost always familiar with the material, but at the same time, it was easy to blend into the crowd if I didn't feel like being the kid with all the answers. There were several high achievers in my class, and for the first time, I was not automatically in the top echelon of students. If I was not on my A game, the teachers rarely noticed, and if my parents noticed, they didn't say anything.

Ninth and tenth grades were a blur, and before I knew it, I was in eleventh grade. We started thinking seriously about college applications, which I didn't have much insight into. I had heard people talking about Ivy League schools and knew this class of institution had prestige in the world outside Brighton Beach. An Ivy League diploma meant I could get my pick of the best jobs, but tuition at any of those universities would cost an arm and a leg, which I figured put them off limits.

I figured right.

I applied to Cornell and was offered a token scholarship, but it would not cover all my expenses. I was admitted to NYU, but with no scholarship offers. My parents suggested I apply to Brooklyn College, which was pretty much the default choice for kids across the borough whose families, like mine, didn't have oodles of money. There was an application fee of fifty dollars, which I was able to pay with the money I earned as a clerk at the local supermarket. To the surprise of absolutely no one, I was accepted and enrolled for the following year.

BROOKLYN COLLEGE

I started Brooklyn College in the fall of 1964 with a plan to major in civil engineering. I had an odd relationship with the discipline—or maybe *inconsistent* is the better word. When I took the engineering preadmission aptitude test, I received the second-highest grade in City University of New York history. I was quite proud of that achievement—that is, until I got my first physics test scores. Somehow, my ability turned out to disagree with my aptitude—and disagreed vehemently. I had completely flunked it, scoring nine out of a hundred. The next test came back even worse. Physics quickly became the bane of my freshman year; that semester I got a D–. I had never seen marks like that on a report card. Even so, the passing grade was more a reflection of the professor's charitable nature than any indication of academic competence on my part.

Across the Pacific, the Vietnam War was escalating. Like most young men at the time, I worried about keeping my draft deferment status; I did not want to fight in the war, and a good way to avoid the draft was to get top grades. But my ambivalent relationship with physics was leaving me vulnerable. A classmate, Jeffrey, mentioned that he had taken Accounting 101 that semester and gotten an A.

"Is the class easy?" I asked.

"Accounting is pretty straightforward and methodical—plus, you're good with numbers. You'll ace it."

His assessment was on the money. I took Accounting 1 the next semester and got an A and kept my deferment. I also aced Accounting 2 the following semester. Compared with physics, accounting was a snap. I took other business courses and did well in them. In my sophomore year, I switched my major to accounting. The world of civil engineering was spared a disastrous practitioner, but its loss was accounting's gain, or so I would like to think.

One of the friends I made freshman year worked summers at the Homowack Lodge in the Catskill Mountains, one of the hundreds of hotels in the area pulling in a predominantly Jewish clientele. My friend's mother managed the hotel's programs for kids and teens, and I set up an interview with her for the position of a teenage social director. (Hey, don't laugh.)

She told me that I would work some weekends, during school holidays, and over the summer and that my charges would be slightly younger than me. I figured I could hitch a ride with my friend, who drove back and forth all the time. I was a little worried about how I'd manage my future charges though, but his mother waved away any concerns.

"You're pretty mature for your age," she said. "The other kids will listen to you, I'm sure. Can you start next weekend?"

I said yes.

I'm glad I did. It was nice to get up to the mountains again and absorb all the fresh air and sunshine people always insisted were good for me. Of course, this was before sunshine was labeled toxic and preparation for a day outdoors required lathering your body in high-SPF sunscreen.

Being put in charge of a group of teens was ultimately a good thing for me; it provided me a sense of responsibility. I had never been in charge of anyone before, but now I would be responsible for keeping a bunch of adolescents safe and entertained for days at a time.

In my first role as a responsible adult, I created a personality that was part summer-school teacher, part older brother, and part teenage social director. I had watched enough teachers in my childhood to mimic their behavior, and I had ample experience in the older brother role.

The teenage social director part was the biggest stretch. I took my cues from the Catskill *tummlers*, who were a hybrid form of social directors and court jesters whom the other Borscht Belt hotels employed to keep guests entertained. These guys hosted exercise sessions, dance classes, and rainy-day crafts groups nearly every evening. They kept guests amused and busy, no matter what.

I was a shy person and more than a little nervous when I met my charges on Memorial Day weekend, 1966. My campers were kids from all over New York City, and nearly all were delighted to get away from their families for ten to twelve hours a day. Like the *tummlers*, I would need to devise ways to keep them entertained, occupied, and out of trouble. Fortunately, everyone was new; there were no cliques or in-groups that could gang up on the runts—or, for that matter, me. I figured if I acted confident, they might buy the act.

"Hey, everybody, come over here," I told the group. "We got a lot of things scheduled for today. Let's get going!"

With no adults around, I let my inner self, at least this new version of it, come through. Smart-alecky remarks that adults reprimanded me for earned me respect from my campers. My off-the-cuff wisecracks seemed to appeal to the rebellious nature of many teens. You might say I got in touch with my inner *tummler*.

I also met a lovely girl up at the Homowack. (Did you ever see the movie *Dirty Dancing*?) Sheila was a little younger than me, sweet, lively, and charming. Before long our relationship had evolved beyond the strict confines of counselor and camper. We began dating when we were both back home: me living in Brooklyn, her in Cranford, New Jersey. Soon we were "going steady," as we used to say back then. We never stopped.

Working at hotels is very different from vacationing at them. I was nineteen and of legal age but really neither a kid nor an adult. But I was big, sounded older than I was (if you didn't listen too closely), and most of the time displayed a serious and responsible demeanor. In any event, Homowack's employees welcomed me into the fold; it was the first time adults had treated me as one of them. Some of my new colleagues were scarcely older or more experienced than I was; others were quite a bit more, shall I say, "mature." In the Catskills, the original Pollyanna would over time have turned into a more jaded version of Joan Rivers.

The counselor gig ended two hours after dinner, when the kids returned to their families. I was left with the late evenings free and wanted to earn more money. Homowack Lodge had customers who needed their drinks served. Supply and demand, as I was learning in my economics class.

"Good evening, sir," I said to a customer. "What will it be?"

"Whiskey on the rocks, *boychik*," he said. "And a Tom Collins for my wife."

Only the lady was not his wife. Mr. Whiskey Rocks had occupied the same stool last week with a different woman he called his missus. Which one was the real wife? Maybe it was the lady he would entertain the following week. Either way, it was not my business.

I had been raised with the belief that Jews don't cavort or drink a lot. Certainly in Brighton Beach they didn't. Or if they did, I now realized, they made sure nobody from the neighborhood saw them. Perhaps they went up to the Catskills for a tipple and a little action. Who knows? I can tell you that at the Homowack Lodge casino, as nightclubs were called in the mountains, there was no shortage of customers.

Between teen camp and adult camp, as I called the casino, I was working twelve-hour days, sometimes longer. Adult camp taught me valuable lessons about work and earning money. Lesson number one: it's all about how you treat the client. Folks were quite ready to share their problems with me. When I listened politely and nodded at appropriate intervals, kept the bar clean, and was generous with pours, they tipped well.

When I didn't, neither did they.

I was paid less than minimum wage, but with the tips, my pay was through the roof. I earned more than $10,000 the summer of '66, which isn't too bad. I eventually used that money to buy Sheila's engagement ring.

At the start of college, I got involved in a fraternity. I had noticed that boys who joined frats had an instant social life, enjoyed friendly relations with sororities, and could field a decent team when challenged to a game. I joined a fraternity known for providing services and raising funds for worthy causes—Alpha Phi Omega. One of the charitable things we did was run a used-book exchange. The exchange not only helped fund worthwhile charities but provided capital liquidity for superannuated educational materials, meaning students could sell their used textbooks and earn money or buy used textbooks and save. Few students in history have not seen clear value in that. The few who did not likely did not attend Brooklyn College.

The exchange was not open all the time, but when it was, I ran it—I was the CEO. I worked between ten and twenty hours a week and had many roles: clerk, bookkeeper, inventory manager, publicist. Advertising was the easiest way, but that cost money.

For the first time in my life, I managed other people. This was a good learning experience too, one entirely different from my Homowack days. I learned a little about patience, a virtue that I don't have intrinsically in large amounts. I learned that when the people who work for you are volunteers, you have to figure out how to motivate them in ways that don't involve paying them. I learned that you will get more out of volunteers by getting them to care about the outcome of your collective efforts. I learned that people sometimes do dumb things and that you can't just tell them they screwed up or they'll quit. I learned you can train people in the right skills and model the right behaviors, and sometimes they learn but other times they don't.

I learned that sometimes the best way to get something done is to do it yourself.

My little team did several hundred thousand dollars' worth of business. At the end of my first year managing the exchange, we showed a profit of nearly $20,000. We saved thousands of usable books from being shredded and helped students afford textbooks they might not have been able to otherwise. Until you've been at a city college in September and February, the start of semesters, you don't know the meaning of the term *impoverished student.*

In my senior year, I handed the job of running the exchange to an underclassman and started looking for work in my field. The job I found convinced me I would eventually have to become my own boss.

CHAPTER 4

HALPERN, GOLDSTEIN & COMPANY

Early in my junior year, I found a "help wanted" ad posted on the wall outside the Brooklyn College placement office. The prospective employer, Halpern, Goldstein & Company, was a small CPA firm located at 26 Court Street in Brooklyn. The firm consisted of two partners, one accountant, and a secretary. The partners were looking for a junior accountant to work part time. After finishing class, I went over to their offices one afternoon for an interview with Seymour Goldstein and was hired the next day.

I started working several hours a day, several days a week. Most of their clients were plastic manufacturers, apparel firms, and small printing companies. I was assigned overflow work. The firm's largest account, a manufacturer called Gilbert Plastics, located in Kenilworth, New Jersey, landed on my plate. Milton and Sidney Ostrowitz, the two brothers who owned Gilbert Plastics, had put Halpern, Goldstein & Company on notice. As is customary in accounting, you have to continue serving clients who are cutting ties with you, even while they look for new accounting firms, so my employer must have figured that this was a low-risk assignment for a green accountant.

I enjoyed practicing as opposed to studying accounting. Although I was a good student, I preferred actually doing accounting work to memorizing processes, writing papers, and performing other academic tasks. Henry Halpern and Seymour Goldstein were the first accountants I knew, outside of my professors and the moonlighting accountant who visited my family every April to do their taxes at the kitchen table.

If there was a patent on the stereotypical New York accountant, both Henry Halpern and Seymour Goldstein would have been sued. Halpern, who was also a lawyer, owned five suits, which he rotated every day of every week, fifty weeks a year. The suits were equally shiny and the cuffs equally frayed. The man was cheap beyond belief. Anything of value in the office—and many things of no apparent value—was kept behind lock and key, and Halpern held the keys. This included the copy machine. I had to justify every copy I wanted to make, and when I'd ask to use it, he'd usually wave me away dismissively.

"Make the copy by hand," he would say. "What did you do before they invented copiers?"

"I don't know," I would respond. "What did you do before they invented paper?"

Seymour Goldstein was a little younger but cut from similar cloth—probably burlap. I worked there for seven years, and I could count the number of in-depth personal conversations I had with either man on one hand, with fingers to spare.

But I tried to make conversation a few times.

"So do you have any children?" I asked Goldstein one afternoon.

"No."

I was out of conversational gambits, so I said, "Oh? Why is that?"

Without pausing, he said, "Children are expensive."

There's a joke accountants tell: an extroverted accountant looks at your belt buckle instead of your shoes. Goldstein told me that joke; it was the first time—and last time—he never told me a joke. When I hear that joke today, I think of my old boss.

He only ever gave me one bit of advice: always tell the client no.

"Whatever they say, you say no," he explained. "If it turns out badly, you say, 'I told you not to do it, remember?'"

"But what if it turns out well?" I asked.

"By then they'll have forgotten what you said."

I liked getting out of the office. I traveled a lot for audits. One time I traveled to a warehouse in Opelika, Alabama, for Gilbert Plastics. Their inventory of plastic raw materials was stored in sixty-foot silos. I climbed the narrow ladder up to the top of the silo and peered in. I threw my leg over the side and began descending for a closer look.

"Boy, what you doin'?" a warehouse worker yelled. "Don't you know there are rattlesnakes in there?"

Maybe there were rattlesnakes in there, and maybe there weren't. I decided not to find out empirically.

Back on the ground, I learned from warehouse management that one of the silos was full and what that meant in terms of storage weight. I went outside; found a few large, similarly sized stones; and returned to the silo. I threw the stones at its side, starting at the bottom and moving up the top. Boom! Boom! The reverberations were consistent. Now I knew what full sounded like. I memorized the sound and turned to the other silos. I gathered more stones and threw them at each silo, and from the reverberations, I determined how full—or empty—the silos were. To make sure they had stored the right materials inside, as opposed to substituting water or sand, I asked employees at random to run out and unload fifty pounds or so. I examined the materials to assure myself the contents were labeled legitimately.

In my report, I mentioned I had formulated a new type of inspection, which I called "sonar auditing." Imagine the advertisement: "Sonar Auditing: No Climbing. No Snakes. No Drama." I should have taken out a patent.

Fortunately, the client seemed to like my work. In the not-too-distant future, the Ostrowitz brothers would play a major role in my career progression. I was glad I had stayed on good terms with them.

CHAPTER 5

MY EARLY CAREER

I graduated from Brooklyn College in June 1968 and without taking a break started full time at Halpern, Goldstein & Company. My biggest account was still Gilbert Plastics—they had liked my work, and their termination notice was forgotten. Milton Ostrowitz, part owner of Gilbert Plastics, was the older and more controlling sibling. Sidney, the other owner, was nice but afraid of his brother. The brothers were very successful in a notoriously low-margin and capital-intensive business. Sidney died in 1988, and Milton had died a few years earlier.

As mentioned in the previous chapter, my bosses "gave" me the Gilbert account after they had been put on notice. By the time I came on board full time, Halpern and Goldstein were barely on speaking terms with the brothers Ostrowitz. Milton and Sidney didn't think much of Halpern and Goldstein either. Goldstein especially was intimidated by them; he managed his company constantly in fear of losing clients. They sensed this and thought less of him for it. As the accounting firm of Gilbert Plastics, Halpern, Goldstein & Company didn't adequately service the client and did not accommodate their growth as the company expanded from New Jersey to California and Illinois.

Because I was neither Halpern nor Goldstein, the Ostrowitz brothers seemed to like me. It was an unusual situation in that Gilbert Plastics did not have a CFO and expected their CPA firm to fill that role. My initial work involved finishing up the prior fiscal year's taxes but grew to negotiating with their raw material suppliers and their labor unions and overseeing their financial and insurance needs.

Like many clients, the Ostrowitz brothers liked seeing the people who provided them with services face-to-face. I think they were old school in the sense that they felt the more they saw you, the more honest and hardworking you'd be.

While the Ostrowitz brothers valued an interpersonal connection, Goldstein and Halpern were dismissive of it. They visited their clients only under duress; they really disliked doing it. I quickly realized that they were shortsighted in this matter.

I, however, held no such qualms; I visited Gilbert Plastics' New Jersey operations often. We spent quite a bit of time over lunches or dinners or smoking Cuban cigars Milton provided. They also introduced me to a broader world than Brighton Beach and Brooklyn: Peter Luger Steak House, Gucci, Beverly Hills, first-class air travel, Cadillacs, hotels (not motels, which I was used to), stone crabs, and on and on.

One happy coincidence was that Sheila lived with her family in the town next to their New Jersey plant. The arrangement made it very easy for me to see her, and that brought me much joy.

Gilbert Plastics was growing aggressively by acquiring smaller companies, many of them competitors and niche businesses. This strategy expanded their footprint and produced a lot of work for an accountant. I did what they asked me to do, all the while peppering them with questions and learning about how they were handling acquisitions, managing mergers, and so on.

It never occurred to the brothers to think strategically about their deals. They cut every corner, but they did not pare down redundant staff as part of the integration process. The deals usually swallowed competitors, brought in new customers, and eliminated the costs and inefficiencies of competition. That was good. The deals also added physical inventory, expanded capacity, and bloated payroll. That was not so good. I gingerly began suggesting ways to handle integration more efficiently.

For example, like most plastics manufacturers, the Ostrowitz brothers bought their raw materials from big petroleum companies. Every year they would negotiate deals with their main suppliers, one of whom was Standard Oil of Indiana, since renamed Exxon. Negotiating with Standard Oil was like David negotiating with Goliath, only more lopsided.

In the past, the brothers had gone to the supplier's corporate headquarters and negotiated terms for the coming year's supply. After I had handled their account for a few months, to my surprise they sent me alone—and I wasn't even a CPA yet.

Other than allowance haggling, this was my first experience negotiating. I imagine that, as I sat across the table from a team of highly paid corporate people in a conference room in the Standard Oil corporate headquarters, I did not strike anyone as particularly intimidating. On the other hand, it never occurred to me to be intimidated. I had learned a little concerning negotiations about market pricing, deal finance, and which terms were variable and which were not. I didn't steal the rug out from under Standard Oil, but on the other hand, they didn't eat me for lunch either.

When I returned to New Jersey, I presented deal terms to the brothers. They said very little, but their faces were glowing.

"You know, David," Milton said, "you negotiated a very nice contract."

"Thank you."

"You got concessions we never thought of even putting on the table," he continued. "How did you do it?"

"I don't know. I just did it."

I also went on the road to visit companies the brothers were considering acquiring. I would work on pro forma balance sheets, normalize income statement adjustments, determine valuation of their target companies, figure out the cost of acquisition finance, and so on. These were methods I had learned in the classroom that immediately came in handy.

Sidney Ostrowitz was implacable; he simply did not react to what was going on around him. Once Sidney and his wife, Barbara, dined at a steakhouse with Sheila and me. I noticed that while the three of us were making stabs at conversation, Sidney's wife was eyeballing the table next to us. Sidney paid no attention to Barbara and kept eating. When the couple at the table had finished their meal, Barbara said across the table, "Excuse me. Do you mind if I suck on your (lamb chop) bones?"

The couple looked horrified. Sheila turned green, and I felt sick inside. Barbara reached over and grabbed the nearest plate.

Sidney didn't bat an eye.

When I started working full time at the firm, Halpern and Goldstein assigned me several minor accounts. I found them to be mostly small companies that thought small. Their owners were more likely to focus on saving five cents an hour in labor costs than investing in new technology or deepening relationships with better customers. Halpern and Goldstein were the same way. Like accountant, like client.

We had clients like Mrs. Keck. Mrs. Keck—I don't recall her first name—was disabled and homebound, at least as far as meeting her accountant was concerned. She lived in a neighborhood that was never great and was, as she always said, in the process of getting worse—it was a long process. She had had a new fence built and kept the gate securely locked, the better to keep out intruders.

That gate, however, also kept out accountants. Halpern had gotten the account during World War II. In later years, he handed it to Goldstein, his junior partner. In 1968 Goldstein handed it over to me. I soon found out why. Mrs. Keck had limited mobility—and only part-time help to assist her around the house. My first visit was apparently one of the times she was by herself. She called to me from the window. It was the accounting version of "Yoo-hoo, Mrs. Bloom" from the radio show *The Goldbergs*.

"Climb the fence and come in," she hollered. I clambered over the fence, entered the house, took the information to prepare her returns, and went out the way I came in. I was not one of Brooklyn's better fence climbers, by experience or inclination, and tore my suit in the process. When I mentioned this to Goldstein, no offer of reimbursement was forthcoming.

The following spring, I made the same trek, encountered the same locked gate, and received the same invitation from Mrs. Keck to come in—via the same obstacle. Honed by experience, I swung my leg over the gate and gained entry unscathed.

However, on my way out, I repeated the process and once again managed to tear my suit.

When I got back to the office, I was boiling mad. You shouldn't need to put in for combat pay when you do spreadsheets for a living.

"My suit's ripped again," I told Halpern. "Want to know why? I had to climb a fence to do Mrs. Keck's returns."

"Just sew the suit," he said. "What's a little tear?"

"I'm not sewing the suit; I'm buying a new one. Why the hell are we doing all this for $100?"

"She's disabled; she can't come here," Goldstein said. "Also, her husband was a big shot at Lincoln Savings Bank."

"He *was* a big shot," I shot back. "Now he's a *deceased* big shot."

"A very good man," Halpern said. "May he rest in peace."

Goldstein added, "He was good for business."

"Did we ever actually get any business from him or the bank?"

Halpern shook his head. "No. Maybe this year we will though. Who knows?"

By October 1968, it was time to move out of my childhood bedroom. Sheila and I had found a garden apartment in Somerset, New Jersey. It was a newly built complex more or less halfway between Gilbert Plastics' factory and Sheila and her family's residence.

It was an affordable starter apartment with on-premises parking and a swimming pool. The idea was for me to have a quiet place to study for the CPA licensing exams coming up that November. Sheila would then move in after our wedding, which was also in November. I enjoyed the solitude and extra space for a few days, but then I began to feel a bit lonely and called home a few times. Zaydeh had the room to himself now, but I think he missed me too. Despite my calls home, I had a lot of time to study. About the only interruption I had was when Sheila picked me up to go shopping for things for the house—I had never known so many decisions were involved in buying furniture!

I took three parts of the CPA exam that November and passed. Like my college graduation, it was a bit anticlimactic—there wasn't much of a chance that I would fail. However, I would have to wait two years to take the fourth part of the exam, according to New York State experience requirements, which was done back then in an effort to bolster the qualifications of the people taking the test.

After I had been working at the firm for several years, one Monday Halpern didn't show up at the office. He didn't show up Tuesday either. Goldstein informed the office that Halpern had become ill and was in the hospital. Halpern had apparently given the full set of office copier keys to Goldstein before he left, and Goldstein conscientiously maintained the legacy.

I never saw Halpern again. He officially retired, and I took over the bulk of his clients. He died soon thereafter. Not many people from the office attended his funeral; I didn't even learn about his death until several weeks afterward, and I'm sure that was true for the others as well.

A few months after Halpern's death, Goldstein invited me to dinner and offered me a partnership, and I accepted. The following day, the firm was renamed Goldstein & Wiener—which was the biggest change with the new partnership. Sure, I got a little more money, but I continued with my same clients, and life went on more or less the same.

Until, that is, Goldstein did something so outrageous and shortsighted that I had no choice but to make my exit.

CHAPTER 6

OUT ON MY OWN

Goldstein was chronically insecure when it came to billing; he always felt that clients were on the verge of defecting due to our prices. He was a Depression child and never changed his views about money, even after I started earning him more.

One afternoon in 1975, Goldstein invited me to dinner. The last time he had done that, he offered me a partnership. Obviously he wasn't doing that again, so what then did he have in mind? We agreed to meet the next night at a seafood restaurant down the block from the office.

Over dinner, we made small talk. Goldstein asked a few questions about this client or that one. I maintained my end of the conversation and kept things pretty much about business.

Finally, he puckered up, blotted his lips with his cloth napkin, and then used it to mop his forehead. Satisfied he had prepared himself for the upcoming conversation, he leaned forward and said, "You know, David, you phone your wife in New Jersey an awful lot from the office. Every day, in fact. Did you know that?"

Of course I knew that. Did he think I was an idiot?

"Sheila's my wife," I said. "I call her before I head home. Why, is there a problem?"

He smirked. "Just a small one. You see, these are toll calls. They cost money. I always keep my personal calls within Manhattan. Now do you understand?"

It should be noted to younger readers that during the Stone Age (i.e., the seventies), customers paid the phone company fees based on regional toll districts. This was before internet and phone bills were integrated—in fact, it was before the internet (can you imagine such a thing, kids?).

"Every time you call Sheila, the firm has been paying the bill," he went on. "So to reconcile, I'll just deduct your toll calls from your paycheck every month. Pretty simple, I think."

He leaned back in his chair and took a sip of water, which of course was free.

I stared at him for a long moment, then said, "Exactly how much are these phone calls costing the firm?"

"Glad you asked," he replied. He reached into his briefcase sitting by his feet and pulled out a folder with the month's phone bills. The calls to New Jersey had been redlined. "Let's tally this up."

He took out his calculator, clicked a few keys, and said, "It comes out to about fifty dollars a month."

I knew that our firm's revenue had more than tripled in the short time since I came on board. I can't say the increased business was all my doing, but I was billing existing clients more and attracting new clients through referrals. Goldstein was now earning more than $100,000 a year—a huge increase from $15,000, which was his annual salary back when I started.

I remained calm but said in a low growl, "You son of a bitch."

Goldstein replied icily, "Now, there's no reason to get personal. It's just business."

"I quit," I said loudly. "I'll stay until April 16. After that, I'm done."

My outburst was drawing stares from a couple at a nearby table. I stared back, causing them to awkwardly look away. The bill lay on the table and had already been paid, so I looked. Goldstein had stiffed the waiter on the tip. Nothing new there.

I reached into my wallet and left a few more bucks on the table. The small act of generosity made me feel better. I could—and would—be the opposite of Goldstein.

When I returned to the office, I called Sheila immediately from my desk phone—just to spite Goldstein.

"Hi, honey," she said. "How was dinner?"

She sounded so sweet that for a moment, I couldn't say anything. I cleared my throat. "The fish was delicious . . . and I will be unemployed in a few months."

I was earning nearly $50,000 and was the sole breadwinner for a family of four, soon to be five: Sheila, me, and our children, Paul and Rachel—Laura was on the way.

I heard Sheila gasp.

"It's a matter of self-respect," I stammered. "I can't let him treat me like that."

In the silence that ensued, my words rang in my ear. I knew my decision put us in a difficult situation; my pride wasn't going to pay the mortgage.

Finally, Sheila said, "Good for you. You don't deserve to be treated like that. Screw him. We will be fine."

And with that, I knew everything was going to be all right. Eventually.

CHAPTER 7

ON FIFTH AVENUE

I continued working on the Gilbert Plastics account the rest of the time I was employed at the firm, but all the while, I was planning my new business venture. I would need a partner; I believe that you should never go into business by yourself if you can help it. I found a partner in Sydney Hyman, a Brooklyn-born lawyer who worked out of a small office downtown near Broadway. I worked on many clients together with him and got to know him quite well. Sydney wanted to move uptown, and I was his ticket to do that. He was older than me, and I liked the idea of benefiting from his experience. He'd probably be good for a few referrals too. We both began contacting commercial real estate brokers.

In March, one of the brokers called and told us to meet him at 592 Fifth Avenue, at the corner of Forty-Eighth Street, *immediately* (he repeated that for emphasis).

Sydney took the subway uptown, and I came out from Brooklyn. In short order, we were walking through what seemed like a palace: four thousand square feet of vacant executive space. The walls were covered in teak an inch thick, and the space was adorned with many marvelous interior-design touches, such as built-in cabinets, private bathrooms, rosewood doors, soundproof glass–partitioned offices, a conference room, and so on. There was a terrace looking down on St. Patrick's Cathedral that was bigger than the square footage of my family's Brighton Beach apartment.

It turned out the building was owned by the National Bank of North America. The senior managers had bickered among themselves over who would get the offices connecting to the terrace. In the end, they rented the space to outsiders—it was the embodiment of the line "If I can't have it, no one will."

The unintended beneficiaries of the bankers' inability to play nice turned out to be Sydney and me. It's important to present yourself well to clients, both regular and prospective, and the new office would allow us to present ourselves magnificently.

The rent turned out to be $3,000 a month, including utilities. This was the bargain to beat all bargains. I would never have agreed to pay street price for what a palace like that rented for, and neither would Sydney. When the broker took out the lease agreement, I grabbed it out of his hands, fished a pen out of my suit jacket, and signed before the knuckle-heads could change their minds.

We borrowed $50,000 from a bank and bought desks, chairs, sofas, filing cabinets, a phone system, and even some items to spruce up the decor, and bingo, we were open for business. After nearly seven years working for others, it was exhilarating to finally become my own boss.

In the weeks before I left Goldstein & Wiener, I made it a point to let certain clients know I was opening my own practice. There is nothing more depressing than opening a beautiful, well-staffed office in Mid-town Manhattan—or anywhere, for that matter—and sitting there all day twiddling your thumbs.

Happily, this did not happen.

Milton and Sidney of Gilbert Plastics were not taciturn. They talked a lot about who they liked and who they didn't, and their words carried weight in their industry and community. Thankfully they liked me—they left Halpern, Goldstein & Company when I opened the new business, and Gilbert Plastics became my first substantial client. I started getting calls from their friends and business associates. Now that I was living in New Jersey, I would meet people who knew them at social gatherings and started spreading the word of my new firm. I also met other people who owned businesses in need of an accountant (many of them plastic manufacturers).

One of the other clients that I had worked for at Goldstein & Wiener was Economic Information Systems—EIS. Their two principals, Bent-ley Paykin and Jay Gould, were world-class economists. What's more, Gould was a close relative of Henry Halpern. EIS was in the database and econometrics business, a pioneer in that nascent industry.

Soon after I left, Paykin called me and said he'd like to work with me. I told him Goldstein would not allow it.

"What needs to happen to make this work?" he asked.

"Well, if Goldstein were compensated for losing his $35,000-a-year client, he would probably become very tolerant very quickly," I explained.

Immediately, Paykin agreed to give me $35,000 so that I could pay Goldstein. I was astounded, shocked, and flattered. I now had my second significant client.

Indeed, my first mergers and acquisitions (M&A) transaction involved EIS. EIS was approached by Control Data Corporation, and Jay Gould asked me to work with him on the negotiations. I was able to improve the offer by about 50 percent. EIS was so delighted, they agreed to pay me a $200,000 "success" fee at closing. It would not be the last such fee.

When I returned to New York, I visited a jewelry store on West Forty-Seventh Street. I picked out a Rolex watch for myself and diamond stud earrings for Sheila. I wrote out a check for both and told the store owner not to deposit the check until the following Monday; it was more than what was in my checking account by a wide margin.

The deal went through, and on Monday the check cleared. I returned to the store and left with my new treasures. I still have that Rolex, and my wife enjoyed wearing those earrings for many years until she eventually traded up. If you want to buy a Rolex and you've truly earned it, my advice is go ahead and do it.

I discovered that plenty of business can be found just by attending social functions. I trained myself to chat up strangers and swap business cards whenever possible. It was Homowack Lodge all over again. I even learned how to dance, however poorly.

One of the clients who retained me when I moved to Fifth Avenue was a factor—in fact, it was Gilbert Plastics' factor. Factors are asset-based lenders who take over your receivables and pay you up front, after they deduct a discount. Many factors are fine people. Others are basically loan sharks without the charm. The two brothers/partners at my factor client, Carl and Gerald Grossman, took a shine to me due to my track record scrutinizing receivables. I wouldn't sign off—and still won't—until I was convinced that the company's receivables were 100 percent legit. This made me a hero in their eyes. The partners didn't merely refer me to new clients; they insisted some of their prospective clients hire me. This produced a welcome flow of new business that lasted for years.

The office itself was a delight, and there was plenty of room for staff. Sydney had two attorneys working for him. We shared a receptionist. I hired two staff members: another accountant and an office manager. The accountant was an old friend from Brooklyn College, Bruce Baron. Bruce had graduated as an engineer, discovered he hated engineering, and with my encouragement, returned to school to study accounting. Then he went to business school and got an MBA.

For my office manager, I hired my younger sister, Ruth. She was not temperamentally suited to the work, but she needed a job and worked hard. Ruth held the position for a number of years until she became ill, at which point our insurance provided disability income and medical expenses throughout her retirement.

It took about three years for the National Bank of North America knuckleheads to wise up about our office space. The lease was for ten years, but we received a letter asking us to vacate the space. Fat chance! I had the lease papers and had already negotiated far bigger deals than this. I ignored the letter until the bank's broker finally approached me to ask what it would take to get us out. I settled for $450,000. My share of the proceeds went right into the bank, and I don't mean the National Bank of North America. This tidy sum was the down payment on the new house Sheila and I had decided to build in Morganville, New Jersey, in the early eighties.

Sydney Hyman and I moved together to two other locations over the years, but I eventually decided that it was time for us to go our separate ways. A few days before Splittsville, I was looking over our expenses and noticed my partner had been making large purchases of office supplies and stationery, among other things. That was odd, given the fact that he was going to relocate very shortly. So I decided I would do a little shopping too: the partnership ended up acquiring a new Mercedes for me. The expenditure exhausted our joint checking account. Sydney discovered the deduction on our last day together.

He smiled sheepishly. "You got me."

CHAPTER 8

JAY CHIAT

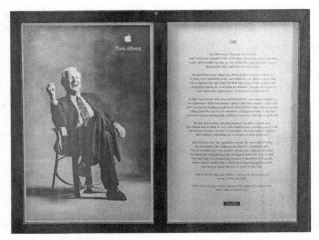

Jay Chiat was admired and loved by the advertising industry.
I had the great fortune to call him a colleague and friend,
and I miss him tremendously.

As mentioned in an earlier chapter, I met Jay through his sister. At a party, I met a client's wife, who happened to be the sister of Jay Chiat, the brilliant ad exec. She asked if I knew Jay. "No," I said, "not really." We'd met at a couple of Christmas parties and exchanged hi-how-are-yous. She insisted I phone Jay and introduce myself. She must have sensed we'd get along.

One day, Jay shocked me by asking me to join Chiat/Day's board. I refused at first.

"Give me six months," he said. "Let's see how it works."

Six months begat another six months, which begat yet another six months, and so on. I ended up staying on the board until I helped sell the agency to Omnicom some thirteen years later. I never found out why Jay offered me a board seat; that was the way he worked: impulsively, unpredictably, and spontaneously.

His method could be described as "ready, fire, aim." He managed his agency like a riverboat gambler navigating the Mississippi. He'd often assert a position so powerfully, no one would dream of challenging it, only to state the exact opposite half an hour later. If you commented on the contradictions, he'd grin. Mercurial? He defined the term.

Jay started his agency in the early sixties and then hooked up with Guy Day to form Chiat/Day in Los Angeles in 1968. He and Guy were polar opposites—Guy cool as a cucumber, Jay hot as a tamale. In many ways, they counterbalanced each other. Guy was aloof, creative, analytical—never the warmest of human beings. It was obvious that Guy deferred to Jay. Guy's name was on the door, but he was definitely second banana.

Jay could suck the air out of a room, and Guy must have felt oxygen deprived. Guy had left the agency a few years before I entered the picture, but he eventually returned to the fold as a part-time consultant. By that time, Jay had expanded the company, solidified its reputation for groundbreaking advertising, and opened offices in New York and other cities.

Due to Jay's charismatic persona and the agency's growing reputation, Chiat/Day was securing new business almost daily. Its client base included Nike, Drexel Burnham, Yamaha, and a young company called Apple Computer. Jay pursued and seduced executives and entrepreneurs who shared his philosophy: he believed advertisers should invest in understanding their customers—he pioneered account planning in this country—and be willing to spend in order to build, shape, or reshape their images and brands. He couldn't tolerate advertisers who trembled on seeing their own shadows.

Jay believed in hiring great creative people and turning them loose, though he didn't always accept their ideas, and when he didn't, he let that person know—he could turn into a pit bull in a heartbeat. At a new business development meeting, I watched him engage in verbal swordplay with an executive whose approach veered sharply away from his own. Back and forth they went, on and on. Finally the executive stood up, excused himself, and headed off to the men's room.

When he returned, he approached his seat and prepared to pick up where he had left off. Jay peered pointedly at the man's midsection, where his fly was dark and damp.

"You want to manage this office," Jay said, "but you can't even manage your bladder!"

Ouch.

Jay liked to say to employees and clients alike, "Let's do great advertising." Employees loved hearing that because that's the goal of every ambitious creative. Clients loved it as well—until they didn't. Jay used to say, "The day I get a new client is the day I start losing the client." Asked what his greatest strength was in business, he cited his skill in losing clients. He was almost proud of it. He believed if you feared losing a client and started compromising your vision, you'd lose both client and vision.

When I met Jay, I told him I didn't know much about the advertising business. My lack of experience didn't deter him at all. He told me to shut up, listen, and observe for a few months; it was, he explained, an easy business to understand. He was right. I found myself spending more time interacting with people and absorbing their perspectives and viewpoints rather than sweating over balance sheets or tax returns. I saw great results there and anywhere people agree to collaborate and share credit.

Following Jay's advice, I observed and listened more than I spoke. Jay realized that I would be a stronger financial manager and a better fiduciary the more I understood advertising and how the ad industry worked. Time seems to have proven him correct.

Jay quickly found multiple ways to make use of me. As a director, I interpreted what the agency's chief financial officer was saying and doing for the other board members and interpreted the board's positions to the CFO. I stayed close to what the CFO was doing and tried to complement him.

One afternoon, I got a call from a longtime employee at the agency who wanted to meet with me. I asked him why, and he said, "Why don't you ask Jay?"

I did. This guy was in financial trouble, and Jay sensed it was impacting his job. Jay had cause to fire the guy but didn't want to throw him out on the street. Instead he asked me to counsel the fellow and help steer him out of his financial straits.

Over the years, Jay sent various fiscally troubled execs to speak with me in confidence. I did my best to counsel all of them and help them get back on sound financial footing. These were people being paid big salaries yet finding themselves many thousands of dollars in debt. Often their financial turmoil was tied to serious behavioral problems: gambling, drugs, and so on.

On financial matters, I served as Jay's internal spokesman. Art directors, copywriters, production managers, and so on can produce brilliant creative works, but most are hopeless with spreadsheets and budgets. Many can't balance their own checkbooks. Ad execs might shine at pitch meetings, but keep them away from negotiating lease renewals. These tasks became my responsibilities. Intuitively, Jay saw how I would be helpful to Chiat/Day and to him. I was able to help Jay rein in expenses, negotiate better terms with a few clients, and years later, be the lead negotiator for Chiat/Day's sale to Omnicom.

Jay was willing to invest in my professional growth. Because of this, I was able to absorb a great deal about advertising. This was a world-class ad agency and an innovatively (if eccentrically) managed business, so I also absorbed top-shelf lessons about writing, art, photography, client management, marketing, human resources, and leadership. Yogi Berra supposedly said, "You can observe a lot just by watching." That was true of me in my early years at Chiat/Day. I was on their premises in New York or California almost as much as I was at my own practice.

I came to love Jay as a brother, but he was a handful and a half to deal with. Balancing his quest for expansion and prominence was a quiet, admirable insistence on innovation, effectiveness, and quality. Jay believed getting big and corporate inevitably led to becoming soft and second rate. Jay used to say, "How big can we get before we get bad?"

I learned a great deal about how to coexist with a visionary by watching Guy and Lee Clow, Chiat/Day's longtime art director, handle Jay. (Guy passed away in 2010; Lee today is director of Media Arts for TBWA/ Worldwide, part of the parent company that bought Chiat/Day.) Both Guy and Lee knew how important it was for someone to act as the "brakes" on a visionary partner's wheels. They showed me how and when to stand up to Jay. Guy and Lee picked their battles, but when pressed, they'd face off and take everything Jay could throw at them. Then they'd give back as good as they got. All three respected each other enormously and took none of the warfare personally. Well, most of the time, anyway.

At Chiat/Day, employees and clients were part of a collaborative effort that produced one of the most extraordinary ad portfolios in history. Chiat/Day's iconic "1984" Super Bowl spot introduced the Macintosh PC. It famously aired only once nationally, but that was all it needed to achieve an enduring cult status. Reversing the conventional wisdom about advertising and repetition, this ad mesmerized audiences around the world, helped propel Apple into the stratosphere, and established the Super Bowl as a forum for show-stopping advertising. It is often called the greatest ad ever made, and it damn well could be.

Jay's pioneering use of outdoor ads converted Los Angeles into a backdrop for Nike advertising during the 1984 Olympics. Writing in *Advertising Age* years later, Randall Rothenberg likened Jay to a contemporary artist. "Persuasion in Jay's hands," he wrote, "becomes postmodern art."

Jay was a fierce persuader, a reflexive opponent of the status quo, and a relentless advocate for perpetual change. Today he'd be called a king of the disrupters. He liked no one to settle in and get comfortable. You felt like a sentry keeping guard in the night, alert to attack. If no one attacked, Jay would.

Jay had a thing about clean desks. He'd walk into the office, which followed an open floor plan, and upbraid the offender: "Clean this mess up or I'll clean it up for you." Sometimes he'd walk away, leaving the offender standing there quivering; other times he'd sweep his arm across a desk surface, pushing contents to the floor.

One Saturday, he called me at home and asked if I could come into the office the following day.

"The office is closed on Sundays," I said.

"Don't worry," he told me. "I have a key. Oh, and wear jeans."

When I arrived the next day, he explained the plan: we were going to throw out all the typewriters and replace them with computers. By Sunday evening, there were one hundred brand-new Apple computers set up at each desk—I know; I did most of the unboxing.

On Monday, he called me. "You should've been here to see everyone's reactions," he said. "It was great! It was like watching a dog after a vet cuts off his nuts and he tries to lick himself."

Jay had a way with words.

One time, I overheard Jay's conversation with a CEO of a major CPG company. Jay had said that the company's advertising was not terrific, but he insisted that he had a great ad campaign that would increase sales. They booked a meeting three days out. I asked Jay what the idea was, and he smiled, shrugged, and said, "I have three days to come up with something."

A year or so later, I decided it was time to introduce computers to my own office. I told my staff on a Friday that we'd start using Lotus 1-2-3 spreadsheets, a precursor to Excel, beginning Monday—no more paper ledgers, no exceptions. I considered coming in that Saturday and pulling a Jay on them, but I thought better of it. There was no need. On Monday, everyone dumped their typewriters and seven- and fourteen-column pads as David C. Wiener & Co. entered the digital age.

Jay always had multiple irons in the fire. No matter how many different business ventures, side projects, or personal passions he pursued around the globe, he managed to keep the separate pieces moving forward. He was invited to two or three events almost every evening, ranging from industry functions to social galas to big-ticket entertainment. People were so eager for him to appear, they sent him complimentary tickets. Often he'd invite me, I suspect to keep him company and fend off glad-handers. Or maybe he just liked my company.

One evening at an awards gala, as we dug into steaks, he stood, excused himself, put his napkin on his seat, and walked off toward the men's room. He never came back—not even when the evening's honorees were called to accept their trophies.

This was the time before cell phones, so I had no way of contacting him. When I got home that night after the ceremony, I dialed his home number. Then his second home. He finally picked up when I called his third home number—third time's the charm.

"Where the hell were you?" I asked.

Jay responded calmly, "Sorry about that. I really wanted to be out in the Hamptons tonight. So I just kept going."

"Of course you did," I said, shaking my head. "I should have known."

"David, listen to me," Jay said. "These events will suck up your life. There are too many of them. Take my advice: make your appearance, maybe have a cocktail or two, and then leave."

Jay lived by his own rules—and I guess we all lived by them too, on some level.

Jay never did anything simply. He threw himself into all he undertook with a passion he couldn't control—and you couldn't help but share. He fell in love with things, places, people, and ideas, sometimes all at once. And they often fell in love with him too. He was seductive that way.

Jay's passions were like him: unpredictable, various, and all consuming. In the late eighties, he fixated on creating a small trading company that would do business with the Soviet Union, beating corporations like PepsiCo and Philip Morris to the punch. He got the idea into his head that the country needed a chain of sandwich shops with a unique design to attract customers. He hired megastar architect Frank Gehry, who also designed Chiat/Day's Los Angeles office, to design those shops. Both the sandwich shops and office building looked impressive, but neither had an efficient use of space. It was like hiring a five-star chef to make you coffee and bagels with a schmear every morning. His gamble did not pay off; the country had very little interest in these sandwich shops, and the business was closed.

These investments cost money, of course. Jay had a way of coddling people when he needed investors. Torg, our trading company, lost money; the sandwich shops lost money; and the Frank Gehry office building disappointed financially, if not aesthetically. A number of senior Chiat/Day executives participated, and let's say there were write-offs. Jay's response when investors lost money? "Come on, people, what's the matter with you? We had a ball!"

Chiat/Day was a juggernaut for most of the eighties. The agency went through a leveraged buyout in 1988, which added to its debt load. The following year, Jay achieved his desire to go international by acquiring Mojo, an Australian agency, which also added to the company's debt load.

By the early nineties, I began talking with Jay about the wisdom of seeking a buyer for the agency. I believe to this day that agency owners who choose their buyers carefully and negotiate well bring their agencies to new levels not possible through organic growth. I mentioned to Jay Goodby, Berlin & Silverstein's recent deal with Omnicom and cited the likely benefits: being the chairperson of a true international agency, Chiat/Day's financial freedom, and more personal time for Jay to travel and pursue his passions.

Jay's response? "Shut up. That's crazy."

I brought it up again a few weeks later. This time, Jay made a face and said nothing. By the third time, he relented: "Who are you thinking about in terms of buyers?"

I had already given the matter some thought. The name at the top of my list was Omnicom. Omnicom was—and is—one of the best and most creative holding companies. What's more, it had a growing appetite for deals and had been acquiring highly creative ad agencies left and right. I set up a meeting, and though nothing tangible came from it, Jay and Omnicom agreed the idea was viable and that we'd meet again.

Omnicom was not the only suitor. Jean-Claude Boulet was an extremely charming French advertising executive who wanted to merge his agency, Boulet Dru Dupuy Petit, with Chiat/Day. Boulet's agency, which eventually was renamed BDDP, had been very successful in France and was hot on entering the US market. Jay himself was a bit of a Francophile and was definitely intrigued. The two men met at Cannes during the annual ad festival and discussed the plan privately. Eventually the idea ran out of steam and was dropped. Omnicom would end up buying BDDP some years later, and Jean-Marie Dru—the D in BDDP—would eventually run Jay's agency, then named TBWA\Chiat\Day.

Conversations with Omnicom picked up intermittently. Throughout the years, Jay and other senior Chiat/Day executives and board members would meet with Omnicom's top people. Finally, in 1995 Chiat/Day was sold to Omnicom.

Jay was gracious in ceding control when Omnicom took ownership. He simply walked out the door and never looked back. Most of the agency's key people stayed on. Today, TBWA\Chiat\Day continues the tradition of great creative work, and Lee Clow, Jay's longtime creative director, is still among the most admired people in advertising.

After the deal, Jay played golf, spent more time in his Marina del Rey townhouse, and dabbled with internet start-ups. By 1998 he was back full time helming an internet company that made and sold web content, working collegially with people a third his age.

Then he was diagnosed with prostate cancer.

We had kept up our relationship since the sale, and I continued to do personal work for him. I didn't bill him for any of it—I just didn't have the heart.

One time at lunch, he told me, "Send me your freaking bill. What's the matter with you?"

"I'll charge you when you're one hundred," I told him.

He took the bait. "Why one hundred?"

"Because that's when I turn eighty-five."

I saw a tear well up in his eye, the only time I ever saw that.

Over time and as his health deteriorated, it started getting harder to reach him. I left many messages, but my calls weren't getting returned, which saddened me. His wife did not like me and blocked my communications with him.

Late one evening, my phone rang at home—it was Jay. In a faint voice, he told me they were starting the morphine drip; he didn't have much time left and was calling a few people one last time. "I love you," he told me. "Have a great life."

I managed to keep my composure the whole time he was on the phone; he never heard me sob or tear up. He passed the next day.

When Donald Trump became president, it called to mind our very own "You're fired" experience. Chiat/Day did the ad work for Harrah's Casino before Trump bought it. After the sale, Jay got a letter from Trump, who wrote, "Your ads are OK, but they're not world class like everything else Trump does." Jay wanted to resign the account immediately, but the Atlantic City regulators said he couldn't resign; rather, he would have to be fired.

Jay knew immediately how to make that happen. He returned the letter to Trump with a handwritten note on the bottom: "Dear Donald, your letterhead was stolen by some asshole."

Chiat/Day was quickly given its walking papers.

Rest in peace, Jay. You've earned it.

CHAPTER 9

MARTIN PURIS

Martin Puris of Ammirati & Puris was one of the top advertising figures for several decades. In the mideighties, we were introduced by a mutual friend. Martin had previously sold his firm to the British agency BMP, which was later bought by Omnicom. I helped Martin—who handled most of the operational and financial aspects of the business—and Ralph Ammirati buy the company back.

In the months that followed our first meeting, I did some consulting work for them and eventually connected them with a bank. The bank agreed to finance the buyback of their firm based in part on the strong case we made for robust future earnings. Some years later, I helped them sell the firm to Interpublic.

Ammirati & Puris was always a class act. The work they produced was elegant, literate, and clever—and insistently brand based. (Unfortunately, not all advertising is; often it is merely clever or attention grabbing.) Martin coined unforgettable campaign slogans for BMW ("The ultimate driving machine"), Club Med ("The antidote for civilization"), and UPS ("The tightest ship in the shipping business"), and Ralph's art direction was the perfect visual complement.

Both Martin and Ralph were gentlemen of the first order. Years ago Ralph told the *Wall Street Journal,* "Good ads cost no more than bad ads. The difference is the strength of the idea." The comment exemplified the vision both men shared. They were equally dedicated to nurturing young professionals and believed their firm should serve as a breeding ground for creative talent. Over the course of many years, I also worked closely with their CFO, Phil Palazzo, who remains a good friend and a current competitor of mine.

At one point in the early nineties, I completed a project that alleviated certain constraints on the agency and allowed the partners to move forward as they wished. Martin thanked me, and we chatted a while in his office. This was just before a three-day holiday, so vacation and travel destinations came up in the conversation.

The next day, there was a slender envelope that arrived in the mail that contained a ten-year membership to Canyon Ranch in Lenox, Massachusetts. The certificate came courtesy of Ralph and Martin.

On another occasion, after I had completed a different project, Martin called me.

"David, thank you," he said. "I can't tell you how much I appreciate your efforts. Now, tell me, what fee would put a big smile on your face?"

"Five million dollars," I immediately said.

Martin chuckled. "OK, then, what price will produce a slight grin?"

"A hundred thousand dollars," I said.

The next day, a case of Dom Pérignon arrived at my office, and taped to the top of the box was a check made out for $150,000.

Martin was—and is—a man of impeccable elegance. His work and living quarters reflect a bon vivant's appreciation for style and design. One day I arrived for a work session at his Manhattan apartment. In his living room, I sat on an armchair, and he took a seat on the sofa. Between us was an exquisite table bearing a bouquet of dozens of vibrant and lovely flowers—I hadn't seen that many since the last time I was at the Brooklyn Botanical Gardens. The vase that held the flowers was an antique and also beautiful. Meeting people like Martin, I had learned to pronounce it *vahze* (rhymes with the Boston-accented word *cars*) rather than *vaze* (rhymes with *haze*).

However you pronounce it, it seemed to take up all our work space. I gestured at the bouquet. "May I move this?"

Martin edged it to the side of the table.

I extracted a work folder and placed it on the table, next to the vase. After Martin inspected the contents of the folder, he handed it back to me, and I returned it to my briefcase and then extracted a second folder. By the time I had leaned over to put that folder on the table, the table was occupied once again by the precious vase.

"It really is a lovely bouquet, Martin, but can we make some room for the next set of documents?"

Martin complied, and the vase was slid back to a spectator position. We resumed our conference.

When this happened a third time, I snatched the vase and walked it over to a table near the window. There it would cast its beauty until the end of our conference. Martin said nothing, but I'm sure it was back on the table before I reached the elevator.

For a number of years, Ammirati & Puris was headquartered on the sixteenth floor of 100-104 Fifth Avenue, just across the street from Chiat/Day. Chiat/Day was also on the sixteenth floor of 79 Fifth Avenue. One day, as I sat in Jay's office, I looked out the window.

Martin waved at me from across the street.

Several days later, I was sitting in Martin's office. Through the window, I could see Jay at his desk.

"David, as you know, I have enormous respect for Jay," Martin once told me.

"So do I. And he does for you as well," I said.

Martin nodded. "Speaking entirely theoretically, suppose I phoned you in the middle of the night, and at the same moment, a call came in from Jay. Which would you answer first?"

"You mean the lady or the tiger?" I asked.

"I'm quite serious, David."

"Jay. I would answer Jay first."

"Is that so. Why?"

"Because I've known him longer."

The next day, his CFO phoned me and said my services were no longer required.

A few months later, the same CFO called and invited me to lunch with Martin. At lunch, Martin told me the guy he had hired to replace me had tragically ridden his bicycle off a cliff. Martin admitted that the dismissal had been ill conceived on his part and that he regretted letting me go. A few days later, his CFO called again and asked me to come back. I said yes. I still work for Martin and Puris & Partners, a marketing consulting group he founded in New York. A world-class creative, Martin Puris is also a world-class gentleman.

CHAPTER 10

JERRY, ANDY, AND THE GANG

I met Jerry Della Femina in the eighties through a referral from Jay Chiat. When we met, Jerry asked me if I knew much about the ad business. I shrugged and explained that I was on the board of Chiat/Day. That seemed good enough for Jerry. It probably didn't hurt that we were both Brooklyn boys who were practically neighbors (he hailed from Coney Island, which is adjacent to Brighton Beach). He asked me to handle a few projects.

Along with George Lois and a rapidly dwindling number of others, Jerry is among the last of the sixties-era "creative revolution mad men" still active, still servicing accounts, still chasing new business. Nearly everyone who meets him falls back on the phrase "larger than life" to describe him. He is among the few figures left in the industry identifiable by first name alone.

Jerry's comment about "advertising being the most fun you can have with your clothes on" has been widely quoted again and again. In addition to his substantial bulk, Jerry projects enormous self-confidence and experience. He started his career as a copywriter for the Daniel & Charles Agency. Through the midsixties, he built his brand while at times butting heads with higher-ups at a series of agencies, including Ted Bates. He and Ron Travisano launched Della Femina Travisano & Partners in 1967 and created popular spots for Ralston Purina (the Meow Mix singing cats), Isuzu (the lying car salesman Joe Isuzu), and Blue Nun wine (with comedians Jerry Stiller and Anne Meara). Jerry bought out Ron and then sold the agency to a British group, WCRS, but stayed on. Eurocom, the French agency, then bought the shop. Jerry fussed with the new ownership, formed new agencies, and went through several new partners. He now heads Della Femina Advertising.

Jerry has an undeniable flair for grabbing attention, especially for himself. He is a virtuoso when it comes to quotability. He is, above all, himself.

Andy Berlin is a man of substantial talent and strong personality. He always said that if you want to do great work, you have to give the client "sweaty armpits"—though not everyone likes the smell of sweaty armpits.

I represented Andy and his partners in the sale of Goodby, Berlin & Silverstein's majority interest to Omnicom. I also represented him in several of his partnerships, his compensation negotiations with Volkswagen, and several of his terminating relationships.

Andy also had the unusual but seemingly brilliant habit of offering to resign his agency's services when a client brought in a new CEO or CMO. He was setting a tone; it was likely not a convenient time for them to change agencies in a transition period like that.

In a way, Andy resembles Jay in that he always was ready to push a creative concept, even if that nudges the client past his or her comfort zone. A serial agency creator and seller, Andy's partnerings and subsequent breakups have been extensively chronicled in the media and widely discussed in ad circles.

Two of Andy's agencies, Goodby, Berlin & Silverstein and Berlin Cameron & Partners, continue to do well today (the former is now Goodby & Silverstein). Andy helmed worldwide ad agency DDB in Manhattan on behalf of Omnicom and was chief executive of WPP's United Creative Agencies Group. He transitioned from advertising into investment banking in the late nineties.

Andy commands a booming voice and enjoyed doing much of the voice-over work for commercials produced by his agency as well as others. Andy is the kind of guy who walks into any room and immediately seizes attention. Today he lives in Charleston, South Carolina.

Saul Waring was a longtime partner with Joe LaRosa, and together they formed the firm Waring & LaRosa. The men epitomized the sixties Madison Avenue scene chronicled in the TV series *Mad Men*. Another Bronx boy who rose to the top during the so-called Golden Age of Advertising, Saul created a niche for himself by creating humorous, sitcom-style spots for brands like Ragu ("That's Italian") and Perrier ("Earth's first soft drink"). Saul and Joe sold their firm to BBDO in 1984. After BBDO merged with Omnicom in 1988, Waring & LaRosa lost their major clients, leading the founders to buy the firm back. They proved highly competitive when it came to winning clients, regaining Fisher-Price toys and landing Progresso after the departure of Ragu and Sunshine Biscuits. I helped them sell their agency to Young & Rubicam in 1996. In later years, they created a nonprofit called the Sagency, where they deployed their considerable marketing skills to bringing art and music to underprivileged children and other projects. It was a worthy idea but ahead of its time. Saul was a sweet man and generous philanthropist whose lifelong habit was to squeeze every dollar bill until the eagle cried. He passed away in 2015. I miss you, Saul.

Donny Deutsch joined his father's ad shop in the early eighties, and by 1989, he was running it. Eleven years later, I helped him sell it to Interpublic for $265 million. His CNBC talk show, *The Big Idea with Donny Deutsch*, gave him national name recognition. I know him as a man of absolute integrity and considerable generosity. After the sale to Interpublic, he asked me what my largest transaction fee ever was. I told him, and he matched it. After the sales proceeds from his agency cleared the bank, he immediately donated the funds needed to pay off the mortgage on the temple in Hollis Hills, Queens, where he grew up.

Donny taught me that a confident person can be tender when appropriate. He treated his dad with incredible love and respect. He is the same way with friends and business associates. When my dad died, he visited my family and joined us during the mourning period of Shiva. Later, after Sheila and I established the Benjamin Wiener Foundation, he quietly made a substantial donation. Behind the media-friendly exterior, Donny Deutsch has an interior of pure gold.

CHAPTER 11

ON FIRING AND BEING FIRED AND OTHER EXPERIENCES

I don't have many small-minded companies as clients. I don't have anything against them, but early on, I realized that your clients define who you are, and I didn't want to be defined by permanently small businesses; I generally do business with successful companies.

When we were at J. H. Cohn, one of my partners brought in a smaller business as a client: Meatball City, a sub shop on the Jersey Shore. It was too small, and it seemed that it would remain that way. I called the owner and told him that we were not specialists in fast food and that the location did not work for either of us. I told the owner that we'd work for no fee until he found a replacement. He told me I was making a big mistake; he was about to open Hot Dog City in addition to his sub shop. I remain comfortable with my decision.

I've fired clients and clients have fired me. I don't enjoy being on either end of the experience, but if you do business long enough, it's unavoidable. When you have to fire a client, avoid lengthy explanations or justifications and act quickly and without animus. As an accountant, I'm ethically obliged to continue to provide professional services to any client I've discharged until they have time to replace me.

Fortunately, this hasn't often been necessary.

The first significant client that ever fired me was Gilbert Plastics. Milton Ostrowitz came to my office one day just before our regular Monday-night dinner. Without preamble, he lit into a series of complaints about my performance, referencing matters that dated back over many years, none of which he had mentioned before. When he came to the end of this list of grievances, he announced that I was fired. I said nothing for a moment and then asked him to leave. That night and throughout the following day, I went over all his complaints in my head, none of which I thought were justified. Why had this happened all of a sudden? I tried writing and calling, but he never got back to me.

Years later, I found out from the son of one of the brothers that the owners had applied for financing and had been told by the lender that they would have to work with a recommended accountant. While it would not have made any difference, being told the truth would have been nice.

The experience taught me that even if you do everything right, you can't be sure things will turn out the way you expect. There is always the x factor: other people, over whom you have no control. I realized too that ultimately business is transactional. No matter how often people tell you they like you and that you're doing a great job, that doesn't mean you have a job for life. Stuff happens. Years later, I would hear Jay Chiat say over and over, "The day I get a new client is the day I start losing the client."

It's a fact of business. I've fired clients, clients have fired me. I don't take it personally anymore.

The silver lining about being fired by Gilbert Plastics was that it opened the door to new, more interesting, and more lucrative clients. I became more aggressive in seeking new clients, networked more, and asked for client referrals—I had more time to do so. And soon after, I was retained by Jay Chiat and Chiat/Day as my first advertising client.

One of the first employees I ever fired was a former nun. She had left her convent a week or two before she joined the practice, and Sydney had hired her after one of our secretaries started her maternity leave. The ex-nun objected to the language we used around the office, a fact she helpfully pointed out more than once. She also insisted on calling me "Mr. Wiener"—I prefer informality; it begets more collaborative work. I really didn't want to fire her, but she wasn't working out, so I thought about how to get her to leave without using the phrase Donald Trump made famous on *The Celebrity Apprentice*.

I asked our second secretary for help in getting the former nun to resign and offered her $500 cash and dinner at Peter Luger if she succeeded. About a week later, the former nun ran out of the office and shouted, "You people are crazy! I quit!"

We never saw her again.

"How did you do it?" I asked the secretary as I paid her the $500 and handed her the Peter Luger gift certificate.

"Ben Wa balls," she said.

It became obvious that people who are paid for their ideas and client service are, in general, better clients than people who have to focus on a nickel an hour in labor costs and $.025 per pound of raw materials.

Like attracts like. I built a reputation as the accountant who understood the ad industry. From there, I began attracting more ad clients. The more you specialize in an industry, the easier it is to add similar clients, and after you figure out one problem, chances are you'll find more uses for that solution; you don't have to keep reinventing the wheel. It's only natural to enjoy the work that is somewhat similar.

Working in the ad industry was and is a hell of a lot of fun. Advertising executives are usually creative people with the gift of gab. They often are seen as thought leaders, people who shape how society functions, and they are leaders in best practices for management. They often meet many famous people and help them become even more famous, casting them in their commercials. When you work in their industry, you get caught up in that too.

Someone once related the advertising industry to *The Wizard of Oz*, when Dorothy enters Oz and the world goes from black and white to Technicolor; once you've been to Oz, it's hard to go back to Kansas.

CHAPTER 12

ODE TO THE ADVERTISING AND MARKETING COMMUNICATIONS INDUSTRY

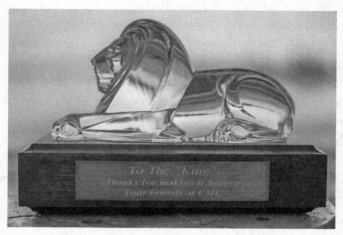

If you equitably owe me money, pay me. Don't give me a fancy Steuben trophy and then expect me to be happy or to forgive your debt.

I enjoy the advertising (or the more expansively defined marketing communications) business for the following reasons:

- It allows people to work together regardless of age, family connections, education, religious affiliation or practices, dress, hairstyle, sex, and sexual practices and preferences.
- The talent, individual and collective, and the ability to communicate, collaborate, and work in a social and intellectually stimulating environment are paramount.
- While the message is quite often intended to sell products or services not always needed, there is a pervasive sense of the need to do it elegantly, ethically, tastefully, and dramatically.

- The "dramatics" can be serious, humorous, and/or visually beautiful.
- It provides a living for many more people than the writing arts, the movie business, the TV business, and other forms of messaging.
- It provides a collaborative way of combining people's talents to mitigate the solitary aspects of many forms of artistry.
- It is a business that quite often recognizes talent and is only slightly less than a perfect meritocracy.
- There are raises, industry awards, peer recognition, and fluidity among agencies that allow for more money, more responsibility, more titles, and bigger clients.
- This is one industry where credentials, a body of work, and industry experience are public and can be used to advance careers—more like acting than surgery.
- The cost of entry is affordable, and new agencies are formed all the time.
- Agencies are sold, combined, and consolidated and make people wealthy more often than they fail.
- Advertising is often used to send messages to improve and correct societal issues—civil and equal rights, political strife, and abuses and wrongs such as bullying, domestic violence, animal cruelty, and so on.
- It promotes positive messages, such as preventing forest fires; the dangers of smoking, drugs, and driving drunk; the benefits of voting; and the need for people to give to charity.
- Advertisers can frequently do it quite emotionally and often for free—pro bono work is more common in the industry than in most other businesses.
- And the good work is not done by force or for PR reasons but is desired, is pursued, and is enthusiastically performed by the staff, especially by younger people.
- Companies use marketing communications for business reasons and to gain and protect profits.
- Indeed, we have recently seen an increase in "cause-related marketing"—combining ads with some good work.
- The business is always evolving.

- It has moved from newspapers and magazines—primarily print—to radio, outdoor, TV, internet, digital, and social media, from mass media to "on-demand" media.
- The industry has moved from observational to participatory, experiential, and cause marketing.
- It has invented product placement, content marketing, and branded content.
- It is evolving from freestanding inserts (FSIs) and mailed coupons to digital and electronic distribution; from purchased media to earned and owned media; from relationship-based engagements to qualitative and results-oriented engagements; from 15 percent commissions to negotiated commissions to fee-based, performance-based, and procurement-negotiated compensation or combinations.
- In addition, the business is an early adopter of new technology and best practices.

Being exposed to the industry has allowed me to see, evaluate, and adopt what is new and refreshing and has stimulated my career and sense of the world. Those early awarenesses have benefited me socially, professionally, and financially and make people think I am smart—for better or worse.

The open-mindedness, inventiveness, and acceptance of ideas and others' expertise provide me with gratifying client service opportunities, financial rewards, and a continuous flow of new projects. I also learned that one can be "creative" in what is viewed as a noncreative field.

Bill Russell "created" a defensive scheme of shot blocking not known before in basketball. One of his great quotes was "The idea is not to block every shot. The idea is to make your opponent believe that you might block every shot."

Surgeons follow protocol and repeat what they learned in training. The "creative" ones modify the procedures and often invent devices to make surgery safer, faster, and more effective. And the inventors often become rich and famous (at least in the medical community).

Marketing services references allowed me the opportunities to work on transactions in other industries—Paul Stuart, Newmark Realty, white-collar criminal defense work, and so on.

My "secret sauce," aside from my client list, is that I tell people I have been doing this since 1981, I know and I am known by the strategic players, and as a CPA, I know taxes, accounting, mergers and acquisitions, and how to negotiate—and by representing so many great creative talents, I have earned a street degree in "abnormal psychology."

CHAPTER 13

LET THE DANCE BEGIN

A DEAL PRIMER FOR SELLERS

The market for advertising agencies and marketing services companies is complex and perpetually evolving. While the market's composition remains consistently dominated by a mixture of financial and strategic acquirers, its dynamics continue to fluctuate. It's a complex dance where the steps are ever changing. Over the course of the present decade, the market's evolution has accelerated.

We'll get into market dynamics in a moment, but first, let's clarify who the actors are on the mergers and acquisitions (M&A) financial stage.

THE SELLERS

Sellers are the agency founders, chief executives, and sometimes the directors and investors who pursue or instigate new ownership arrangements or investor roles for their agencies. Contrary to what many people outside the industry believe, sellers are usually not looking to walk away from their agencies. Rather, most seek to position their agencies for faster growth and expansion into new markets or hope to achieve other benefits possible through new ownership arrangements. Indeed, most sellers remain contractually tied to their agencies postsale by employment contracts and, with increasing frequency, by maintaining minority-equity stakes.

Some executives may be anointed with new titles and be transferred to new locations. Most will be compensated based on their agency's future financial performances for specified periods of time, usually three to five years. That said, a number of sellers are, in fact, looking for exit strategies.

THE BUYERS

Two types of buyers dominate the industry: strategic and financial. Strategic buyers seek to grow by acquiring other companies in their industry. Their focus is on long-term ownership. Strategic buyers are also sometimes called industry buyers. Financial buyers focus on investing. They typically own a portfolio of companies that may have no relation or similarity to what the targets do. Most often their focus is short term.

From my perspective, strategic buyers have become more selective and more strategic in the deals they do. I see fewer deals driven primarily by numbers and far more driven by expected strategic benefits.

Deals used to close primarily on the basis of scale. Company A would combine with company B to produce a new agency, renamed A+B. A+B agency would be significantly larger via a bigger client roster and expanded revenues, have expected wider margins, and so on.

Now buyers insist that deals reflect strategic goals. For example, I recently closed a deal where A bought B primarily because B was a market leader in a niche segment of the industry both served. Creating combinations based on acquiring verticals is increasingly commonplace.

Financial buyers are somewhat more prominent in the marketplace today, making deals to add to their current holdings ("tuckunders") and, importantly, expected resale expectations.

I must say that financial buyers are moving toward transactions with strategic reasons for their expected holding period and to enhance resale values.

In certain cases, large consulting firms acquire companies in order to fill out their credentials and to supplement their consulting, database, and digital capabilities with creative and execution talent. In these cases, they are very much acting as strategic buyers.

With the market becoming more and more strategic, sellers can position themselves advantageously by adapting market-savvy sale strategies. Successful deals leverage client-service capabilities, talent acquisition, enhanced resources, enhanced skill sets, and/or footholds with key clients.

While market multiples have changed only marginally, even for high-quality firms, today there are fewer interested strategic buyers at any one time than was the case in the past. For this reason, deal quality is more important than ever. While the definition of deal quality varies, everyone agrees that a fundamentally sound agency is the sine qua non—Latin for "you can't live without it"—of modern-day deal flow.

The market for buying and selling marketing services companies is decidedly unique. Buyers accustomed to purchasing and selling entities in other industries—for example, casket manufacturers or, dare I say, accounting firms—are likely to find the field remarkably complex. It takes years to understand the industry well enough to visualize feasible combinations. It takes even longer to acquire the skills and personal contacts needed to bring both sides together in a satisfactory fashion and into everlasting harmony—lasting at least until the end of the earnout period. And it takes lots of experience, soft hands, and patience to be able to successfully replace the founders when needed.

The unique financial realities of the advertising agency industry and related fields ensure deal complexity. Cash flows can be byzantine, intellectual property difficult to audit, and agency and individual reputations tough to assess and challenging to monetize—and that's just a sampling.

If you're an agency executive or board member and you're interested in understanding the market, the place to begin is the demand side. Who's interested in buying? The answer will reflect specifically what you're bringing to the market—that is, the quality of your agency, especially the quality and receptivity of the services delivered and the appeal of your client list.

The market for agency deals is both subtle and perpetually changing. To deal successfully, owners must understand what it means to negotiate with each type of buyer in the current market.

As I said earlier, strategic buyers acquire companies to widen their credentials, client relationships, talent base, geographic coverage, and management resources. Their intention is to retain and grow the businesses acquired, to keep well-performing management in place, and to improve operations to better service clients. They often deliver enhanced financial discipline to companies that historically have been entrepreneurial. When A buys B, A expects B to remain a well-managed business and at the same time continue B's presumably high-caliber creative work. B's owners, meanwhile, expect to reap the benefits of a corporate structure—for example, being able to call upon new resources, certain back-office capabilities in administration, and cash-flow management—without giving up the culture needed for creativity. This may include an informal work environment, for example—a some-what indulgent culture where creative types are coddled and are insu-lated from the nine-to-five grind.

Buyers and sellers typically find that, like a marriage, the combina-tion calls for significant flexibility on both parts. Both sides should be upfront during the negotiation process to minimize the likelihood of seller's remorse that sets in all too frequently postdeal.

In my experience, strategic buyers typically recognize and value the cul-ture of the seller and intend to preserve it. How they go about doing that, however, may appear contradictory to sellers. Talented people—exactly the folks whose loyalty the buyer was so eager to obtain—may bristle as administrative and financial discipline is exerted. Goodwill, ample understanding of both sides of the equation, and a healthy sense of humor are absolutely needed to get through the process without doing material damage.

I remember Jay Chiat, who, despite being a creative at heart, would don the proverbial "suit" when necessary, humorously reprimanding a creative: "You started out with an unlimited budget and still managed to exceed it!" As I said, humor is a vital solvent.

Remember, the strategic buyer understands the business the seller is in. In most cases, the buyer has a broad base of experience buying and operating agencies that have performed well, not so well, and all the niches in between. The buyer knows what can destroy a culture and an agency and what can bolster and inspire it.

However, over the years, strategic buyers have acquired so aggres-sively and grown so rapidly that they brim with talent, client rosters, and scalability. Consequently, appetite for the general agency has diminished. Even so, sellers who offer scarce and very specialized skill sets, as well as market-niche strengths, continue to attract great interest.

Several great agencies have thrived after being acquired by strategic buyers / holding companies. They have expanded, increased client bases, become more profitable, and won shelf loads of peer-judged awards. The following are just a few: Goodby, Silverstein & Partners, Anomaly, Crispin Porter + Bogusky, 72andSunny, McGarrey Bowen, DeVries Global, Marina Maher Communications, Cline Davis & Mann, and R/GA.

A financial buyer clearly looks to resell the acquired agency, typically in three to five years. Their usual strategy is to provide capital to fuel growth while imposing strict financial and expense disciplines. Their financial model generally promotes short-term profitability and is intended to position the company for resale. The typical financial buyer often bypasses long-term investments, has little patience for the angst that often accompanies the creative process, and can appear tone deaf in his or her treatment of operating people. Financial buyers can, in most cases, add very little other than capital, M&A expertise, financial discipline, and access to the resale marketplace. The selling principals, used to running their own ships, often find themselves turned effectively into contract workers who serve at will.

Most financial buyer deals are conceived based on economic assumptions that require consistent growth in profits by the acquired agency. Often the financial buyer will not acquire 100 percent of the seller's equity. These so-called rollover deals require the selling principals to "roll over" part of their equity until the anticipated follow-up sale transaction takes place. The seller's ability to cash out even then is subordinated to the debt incurred to finance the acquisition and the return of the financial investor's capital along with a steep preferred return. In these circumstances, the selling principals sometimes find themselves in conflict with the financial buyer's controlling ownership position.

It should be noted that, at times, firms have grown very successfully and rapidly under the auspices of financial buyers that foresaw opportunities to grow in certain niches with their capital. It should also be noted that, at times, the financial buyer sells the firm to a strategic buyer as the company then fits into the strategic needs of the strategic buyer.

This rollover type of transaction with a financial buyer has a very significant difference as compared to that with a strategic buyer: If 60 percent of an agency is sold to a strategic buyer, the seller will likely realize 40 percent of the annual profits each year until the balance of the equity is sold. But in a typical transaction with a financial buyer, since the acquisition is likely to be partially funded with debt, the profits will be used to pay interest and principal on the debt and will not be distributed to the seller. This seems to require a full analytical comparison of the cash flows on an annual basis, the effective multiples, time to full payout, and so on.

One kind of deal structure favored by some financial buyers is the "roll-up," which combines companies for the purposes of making a larger organization—bigger companies, it is argued, often get higher valuation multiples. These mergers combine companies that may not have much more in common other than being part of the same broadly defined industry. These situations are like two people going out on a first date and coming home married—the odds of success under these circumstances are not high.

When planned well by seasoned buyers, certain roll-ups have successfully paired companies and produced synergy—there's that term they love—by combining the resources of complementary organizations. The new, larger companies have emerged as stronger entities in the marketplace and continue to thrive.

The magical words of a successful roll-up are *scale* and *cost efficiencies*. Roll-ups operate on the theory that combinations produce bigger savings. However, since employee costs and rent compose the vast majority of costs in marketing services and shedding staff and space without strategic intent and planning is ill advised or impossible, quite often expectations for significant cost cutting are delusional. Through desperate and ruthless attempts to realize the hoped-for savings, sellers acquired in roll-ups may be surprised at the lack of interest their new bosses have in their culture or even the willingness to maintain and provide the staff and resources to properly service clients. In this way, relationships between buyer and seller go downhill fast. In my experience, such relationships rarely recover.

I believe that the ability to gain purchasing power for inventory and the existence of underutilized or less skilled labor are key to optimizing a roll-up's likelihood of success. Neither of those factors is present in marketing services companies to any significant degree—cheaper staples and coffee cups do not cut it. And I'll make the obvious point here that merging agencies A and B for valid strategic reasons is not a genuine roll-up.

At times, a financial buyer will plan to do an initial public offering (IPO). But for many reasons, this has rarely worked out well in the marketing services arena.

In my experience, very few sellers are prepared to negotiate the sale of their agency effectively. Most are emotionally involved with the transaction and lack the emotional distance, strategic thinking, and financial skills necessary. Most have not thought deeply about their next steps career wise. For example, many are shocked when they learn that a good amount of "their" money transfers to the buyer as required working capital when the deal closes.

Here's where poor account receivable management takes its economic toll on sellers. The slower the billing and collection process, the greater amount of working capital that must remain at closing. Sellers hear that and howl. They should have gone after their chronic late payers a long time before that. Better late than never, I suppose.

Sellers' CFOs, their CPAs, and even their lawyers typically lack the contacts, skills, experience, objectivity, and independence of thought to match the resources experienced buyers bring to the table. Every conversation between a buyer and a seller is part of the negotiation process. Sellers often outline goals, opinions, and positions that complicate or diminish their deal or slim their returns—when buyers talk with sellers, nothing is off the record.

I've enjoyed the benefit of learning the nuances of M&A with some of the industry's premier strategic dealmakers. John Wren, CEO of Omnicom, has taught me that a deal is about much more than money. The seller needs to feel that he or she will continue to be important to the company. The late Fred Meyer, former CFO of Omnicom, believed that paying a good price for a bad business is never smart, but paying a fair price for a good business is always smart. He very much believed in the win-win theory of negotiating and honored the theory by practicing it. I learned quite a lot as well from such industry leaders as Bruce Crawford, Tom Harrison, Dale Adams, Miles Nadal, Phil Geier, Donna Murphy, and others.

CONCLUSION

Agency sellers should prepare for deal discussions by doing the following:

- Prepare—have generally accepted accounting principles (GAAP) financials ready, fix any operating or staff weaknesses, plug any other "holes," and tend to other details. Advance preparation makes all the difference between an agency deal that results in all parties involved feeling positively about the outcome versus one that leaves some players irked, resentful, and certain they were not treated fairly. As an agency sale is often the culmination of many years of effort and investment, taking the time to plan and prepare for entering the market is a worthwhile use of time.
- Retain the appropriate industry-experienced advisers as soon as possible.
- Assess the owners' goals for the company's next phase.
- Assess their own career and personal goals.
- Assess their appeal to the market and set expectations.

CHAPTER 14

NINE STEPS TO A BETTER DEAL

Many of the successful agency deals I do are generated sell-side, rooted in my industry reputation and in my long-term relationships with sellers. In most of these deals, the seller approaches me and asks me to help him or her find and/or negotiate with a group of targeted or interested buyers. I've done so many of these deals over the years that buyers know I bring efficiency to the selling process, and they often recommend me to others interested in selling. Buyers know that though they will pay full retail, they will always be told the truth, and the deal will get done. I'm proud that my business comes mainly through word of mouth—and has for quite some time.

There is a logic to successful deals that both sides sense in advance and that becomes clearer after the dust settles. These deals just seem right. Buyer and seller get along and share a consensus on what's fair and goals for the agency's next phases. The buyer understands and respects the seller's personal and career goals in terms of what happens next, and the seller understands the buyer's economics and business model. They share an understanding of the industry and what's needed to succeed in it. The right people at the agency stay on and become part of the next era, whereas the less talented or more contentious people move on. It's economic recycling.

For an owner first sticking his or her toe in the market, the selling process can be unfamiliar and daunting. The owner of a midsized agency in a midsized market once grabbed me by the elbow as I was leaving his office:

"Remember, David," he said. "I want to make a lot of money from this sale."

"Wait a minute," I replied. "I need a pencil and paper. I've got to write this down so I don't forget."

Pardon my sarcasm, but everyone wants to optimize his or her agency's value. Over the years, I've been asked many times exactly how an agency can do that. Here are nine ways, in no special order:

Step 1. Get to know the buyer. Set up a friendly dinner to develop the deal. In a social setting, both sides can learn quite a bit about each other; when the chemistry is right, everyone knows it. Many deal veterans call this a "first date."

Step 2. Create buzz. As many ad execs and marketing gurus understand, you have to get people talking about your agency. Here are some ways: Create a great updated website. Prepare a credentials presentation deck. Assign your top creative people to your development team. Get yourself invited to keynote industry conferences and speak on panels dealing with trending topics. Offer unique perspectives when you speak. Return any and all calls from trade journalists and advertising beat reporters and columnists. Be your original, captivating, and engaging self when you speak. Get introduced to industry consultants, competitors, and other industry insiders and take them to play golf or to lunch or dinner.

Step 3. Get great clients. Land at least one highly visible, highly coveted account, and do great work for them. Then get a second one.

Step 4. Get great people. Hire the best and brightest and compensate them fairly. A first-class agency has at least two full-time executives on board capable of helming the shop and bringing it to the next level. Recruit and reward them as well as your rising stars. Hire people who have stellar track records and high-caliber personal relationships. Look for people who can book big meetings and help you win big accounts. Recruit top creative people. Identify and hire the best talent available, even if you have to stretch financially.

Cull your agency of dead wood. Identify the people who have been around for a long time and have lost their edge. Reassess their capabilities and reconsider their future at your shop. If it's time for them to move on, make that happen. The people who brought you to where you are now may not be the people to bring you to the next level. No one likes the severance process, but someone has to do it. That someone may be you.

Step 5. Select clients with care. Anyone who opens their checkbook should not automatically become your next client. Cheap clients, timid clients, clients who don't really understand their own businesses, cantankerous clients, unethical clients, and clients looking for personal gratification instead of business advantages are clients you don't need. Show them the door or don't let them in. This advice pertains to professional services firms as well.

Step 6. Rationalize your operations. Are you taking out *too* much of the profit? Pay yourself a fair salary and go easy on the perks. Benchmark your own compensation according to norms in your market. Reinvest some of the profits in the agency on a constant and continuous basis. This means compensating your employees fairly; competitive compensation policies reduce the likelihood your rising stars will jump ship. Pay for the licenses you need based on actual use patterns rather than unrealistically low advance estimates. Invest in upgrading the work environment.

Join the appropriate industry associations and regional business networks. Reimburse staff for the professional training and education they pursue and should be pursuing.

Step 7. Assemble an experienced deal team. Get referrals and interview lawyers and advisors before contemplating any transactions. Don't hire people with little or no deal experience in your industry.

Ask them to elaborate on their experience, and be sure you check all references. Read the trade press regularly. Watch the tombstones—the ads that publicize sales of agencies at completion—to see who's active in the market. Do this early in the process, around the time you first start thinking about your agency's valuation and contemplating sale or exit plans.

If you are not going to retain me, please call me and I will give you a good choice for this step. There is no good #2 choice.

Step 8. Plan your future with *you* in mind. Approach the deal with a clear, realistic, and highly detailed plan in mind for the next five to ten years. Most buyers are prepared to offer you a contract that will extend over the next three years at least, covering the period of earnout.

Determine in advance what title and responsibilities you'd like to have at the new company, who you will report to, and your salary and incentives. Pay detailed attention to any and all noncompete and restrictive covenant clauses and any other contractual restrictions such as those limiting who you can do business with, what industries you can work in, what parts of the country and the world you can operate in, and so on.

Step 9. Do great work. This is the most important step, so let me restate that: do great work.

CHAPTER 15

THE ANATOMY OF A HYPOTHETICAL M&A TRANSACTION IN BULLET POINT FORMAT

HYPOTHETICAL DEAL—START TO TERMINATION

A transaction typically proceeds along the following process:

Meet/Court/Get Retained

I find clients in various ways:

- Client recommendations
- Buyer recommendations
- Lawyer recommendations
- Competitor recommendations (rare)
- Cold calls based on reputation and gossip
- Returning clients

Discuss Seller's Goals

Gather information. Assess numbers; strengths and weaknesses; and accounting, tax, legal, and operational issues. This is often challenging.

Develop a strategy to find appropriate buyers/partners (take into account economics, styles, track record, client conformity, mutual needs/synergies, culture, etc.).

(Discuss auction versus targeted approaches; book to hundreds of prospects?)

Present Summary Information to Buyers

Sign nondisclosure agreement prior to providing confidential information (numbers, client information, etc.).

Arrange meetings.

Negotiate Broad Terms (economic, structural, operational, branding, reporting) and Define Both Sides' Expectations

Broad issues in deal:
- Price formula (amount and timing of payments)
- Tax and legal structure
- Currency (cash, stock, etc.)
- Length of earnout, if any
- If not a 100 percent sale, what happens to the unsold equity in the future?
- Terms for capital investment to grow from buyer
- Incentives to staff and principals to stay during and after earnout
- Issues with clients (present and prospective); who must be avoided
- Holdbacks, etc.
- Representations and warranties from seller
- Buyer's resources to close and pay
- Cap on price, if earnout
- Seller's operational and profit protections
- Profit defined (imposed costs, intercompany charges, intercompany pricing for shared clients, etc.)

Due Diligence Commences (legal, financial, IT, HR, key personnel issues and agreements, clients, etc.) Once Terms Sheet or Letter of Intent (LOI) Is Signed

- Due diligence issues that are not often expected include the following:
  ° Unlicensed software
  ° Poor insurance
  ° Employee promises not in writing or intended to be kept
  ° Overtime and independent contractor versus W-2s (employees?)
  ° Filings in foreign states

Negotiate and Sign Legal Documents

Close Transaction

Press Release

- Must be true, concise, and appealing to all stakeholders and prospective clients

Postclosing

- Tax returns for seller, assist with earnout calculations, adjustments as of closing, changes to deal due to seller and/or buyer, and so on

At times, I assist sellers' principals with financial, tax, and estate tax planning. Each step has had good and bad and expected and unexpected events and issues.

Buyers participate in many transactions and have staff dedicated to M&A, whereas sellers do not have such staff and most often have no prior deal experience, so it is a given that almost all buyers have more experience, more objectivity, and better advice than the sellers.

Sellers often have the following:

Inexperienced lawyers (do not have transaction or industry experience; self-interest takes over, since they will likely lose a client)
- Lawyers have in the past attempted to neuter my engagement letters, removing clauses that protect my economics as an adviser (nonexclusive, no tail, cap fees, list potential suitors, etc.).
- Lawyers have charged high fees ($300,000) to negotiate the deal.
- Lawyers often have a fear of the unknown (earnouts, forced pitches, demand buyer does not compete with seller, etc.).
Inexperienced accountants, internal and external (same issues as the inexperienced lawyers, plus their work/advice is often poor and

careless and is now being scrutinized by me and then by a buyer
during due diligence)
- Cash basis, tax minimization versus profit maximization,
  normalization of results, GAAP, QuickBooks, closing of books
  during the year, multistate filings, "soft costs," top line are fees
  and commissions (F&C) not pass-throughs for media and
  production, market-level compensation for principals, etc.

Brokers who installed inadequate or inappropriate insurance cover-
ages (advertisers' liability, workers' comp, multistate conformity,
general liability coverage, HR coverage, etc.)

Real estate brokers/lawyers who did not check for assignability of
leases without the landlord "extorting" tenant/seller for consent
(issue with lawyer's prior work versus dilutive to public buyer, etc.)

Unrealistic expectations—price, terms, buyer "giving them business,"
"friend said he got . . . ," what is multiple (versus what is multiple
multiplied on), need for transaction to be accretive versus dilutive
to public buyer, and so on.

I need to point out the market value, peer metrics, view of their client
list, work, and need for a distinctive offering (talent, client list, niche, geog-
raphy, etc. are very important factors in establishing appeal and value).

Working capital needs: sell or not, money is "stuck" in the business
Need to pay off debt
Issues with client concentration
- Validate integrity in operations (credits to clients, no hidden
  markups).
- Assess investments in the business and nonrecurring events
  (severance, recruitment, new printers, etc.).
- Discuss how margins/profits can be increased ("anyhow" theory,
  scope creep, etc.).
Risks of client concentration
Need for transparency
Overtime and 1099/W-2 issues

Under my M&A fee structure, I am paid when my client is paid, and the more he or she gets, the better I do.

Agencies that do not make money want their agency valued based on revenue when the market is based on profit.

Agencies are often terminated by their clients when the client's CEO or CMO is fired, even if awards were won and the campaigns were effective.

Good CFOs pay for themselves many times over.

It is incredible to me that an ad agency, whose very value is in ideas and intellectual property (IP), would use pirated illegal software.

I have seen countless problems and lawsuits only because appropriate documents were not signed or properly prepared.

The "anyhow" theory on costs is bogus. To argue that I have the staff, the space, and the infrastructure in place "anyhow" and thus you can reduce your fees to very low levels is destructive and unfair to your staff and to the clients who are paying you the right amounts.

Privately held companies have to have their financial statements "normalized" to accomplish several goals. They should be restated, as needed, to be under generally accepted accounting principles (GAAP) or the international financial reporting standards (IFRS), to reflect costs that are at market levels with up or down adjustments, to reflect transactions that would not have been on the books had an unrelated party owned the company, and so on. Onetime, extraordinary, or unusual expenses can also be added back to profits.

That last line opens up discussions in many fascinating areas by "creative" agency people. The following are some of those discussions:

- The buyer has space and people, so let's add back my rent and administrative people.
- The severance I paid should be added back because those people did not work out.
- My salary should be added back so I can maximize my profits.
- Add back insurance benefits, bonuses, and profit sharing; I will eliminate them after closing.
- Do I need to have holiday parties and other employee perks?

- The recruitment costs I incurred are onetime events.
- The new computers and printers I bought are onetime costs, aren't they?

I could write my second book on this section, but I hope you get the idea. The easiest way to deal with difficult/unreasonable buyers is not to deal with them. Alternatively, one needs to have another potential buyer and compare the proposals. Of course, I need to make my client (the seller) aware of unfair or unreasonable positions and advise on walking away or for the principal to appeal to his or her counterpart on the other side—principal to principal. The top decision makers often need to speak directly to overcome obstacles.

At times, the negotiator is instructed to change certain positions.

Often, showing a buyer a competitor's wording will gain a compromise on certain points.

Sometimes the "difficult" buyer will pay a higher down payment or "seduce" a seller into a deal.

At times, I see a buyer who has limited capital and no understanding of the market or valuation and wants to transact. The approach I take is to educate him or her, give examples, assess his or her financial ability, and see where it can go as soon as possible.

While I do not like doing it and it is contrary to my typical way of doing negotiations, I will take outrageous positions or stances and then have those to "give away" while trying to gain some greater degree of rationality.

I do have a substantial advantage in that I often represent attractive companies and my experience is broadly known.

Lastly, I try to appeal to the person's sense of fairness, and almost all M&A people really do know what is fair or not. Of course, it will not always succeed, but it is telling to the seller, my client, when something simple is unfair and allows the seller to walk away from a particular buyer. Buyers also have to carry the burden of busted negotiations, unhappy deals, and unfair positions, and it impacts them, to a degree, in a relatively small and communicative marketplace.

An interesting observation I have on the economics of marketing services companies relates to the amount of work they perform for a client for a fee.

The scope of work (SOW) for a project-oriented business is fairly clear and specific, the compensation is negotiated, and it is the responsibility of the agency to manage resources within the fee to make a profit.

While a project-oriented business has challenges in the area of managing staff with an irregular income stream, the work for payment is readily managed and mostly automatic.

The project-oriented company will most likely ask for additional compensation as the SOW increases.

An agency relationship that is broader—perhaps an agency of record (AOR) contract—has a major challenge in that the SOW is not typically clearly defined and all of the client's needs or requests are likely demanded to be provided.

The client-service person will be more sensitive to keeping the client happy over the economics.

It is probable that the compensation is based on head count (full-time equivalents [FTEs]) and not based on or flexible to accommodate an increased workload.

The result is more work for a tightly defined number of people without any additional compensation, which equals lower profits, more stress, lower quality of output, fewer happy clients, and so on.

In my experience, sellers never have a difficult choice to make between buyers; one always shines through, whether it is because of price, terms, chemistry, strategy, or feel. There may be a hard choice whether or not to close, but that is a personal or emotional issue, for the most part.

Working in the advertising and marketing communications arena brings me opportunities and experiences I'd never otherwise have. I see creative ideas and cultural intelligence, and I get close to some of the most creative people in the world. I learn how other people think, how to appeal to emotions, and how people use certain skills, and I continuously try to develop and feed off their energy. And many of them respect what I do, at the same level of respect I have for what they do.

Agencies sell for a multitude of reasons—never is the combination the same: greed, necessity driven by clients, need for capital, aging of the principals, opportunity to play on a larger stage, buying out partners, correcting overexpansion and the financial ills, or personal liquidity (boat, second home, divorce, overspending, etc.). One of my clients needed to sell because he was ill and needed cash to pay off debts and medical bills; another was an estate where the principal suddenly died.

Often sellers spend their newfound liquidity in a wasteful manner; they do not recognize that their income is going to be reduced as a result of no longer owning the business. Selling at a multiple and, of course, paying income taxes on the sales proceeds leave the seller with a material amount of liquidity. But a prudent investment yield is going to be less than the profit enjoyed prior to a sale. An illiquid, somewhat risky asset can be converted to liquid assets, and a conservative investment portfolio will yield much lower income. Spending much of the sales proceeds on costly assets (boats, planes, homes, horses, etc.) exacerbates the economics as well.

CHAPTER 16

WORKING WITH LAWYERS—SOME GOOD, SOME NOT SO GOOD

A jury consists of twelve persons chosen to decide who has the better lawyer.

—Robert Frost

Over the years, I've encountered, collaborated with, argued with, and told off enough lawyers to form a bar association for a midsized city. Not every lawyer is dreadful, of course. To be sure, there are many conscientious and stellar attorneys. With them, I have no problem. Other counselors seem to have "Problem" as their middle name. These people are the bane of my existence, genetically programmed to throw wrenches into otherwise sound deals. I can almost smell them when I enter the room.

The best deal attorneys know their stuff, understand the laws involved, and understand the customs that govern deal-making. When I have problems with lawyers, most of the time they're practitioners who do occasional deals and think—erroneously—that they know what they're doing. The less they know, the more aggressive and uncompromising they become.

Once I was sitting across the table from a lawyer who does deals about as often as Halley's comet passes. It seemed like he tried to redline every word containing vowels. One clause in particular seemed to get his underwear in a twist.

I'm not the most patient man in the world, so I finally said, "The clause stays. It's perfectly legitimate, equitable, and customary."

His face turned red as he shouted, "Did you go to law school?"

"No," I said coolly. "Did you?"

I was midway through a deal involving the sale of a New York–based midsized ad agency to a much larger firm. When the draft document came back from the buyer's lawyer, it contained a restrictive covenant, which happens all the time, but this one was strange. It specified the sellers' principals couldn't practice their craft in Venezuela or Costa Rica. Neither of the owners could so much as say "Hola," nor had they given any indication they planned to set up shop in South America. The covenant seemed to make no sense, except for the possibility that the buyer's lawyer mistakenly applied a clause intended for another deal. It was a careless "cut-and-paste" error.

As a courtesy, I phoned the lawyer and politely suggested the clause might have been a mistake. She immediately screamed, "There's no mistake. I won't make any changes!" and then hung up on me.

The deal moved forward. After closing, the lawyer called me and brought up the covenant.

"What's this doing here?" she asked. "There must be some mistake."

"Remember I called you about this? Your exact words were 'There's no mistake.'"

My clients honored the covenant in letter *and* spirit. They stayed out of Venezuela, Costa Rica, and, indeed, the United States for the duration of the restricted period.

Of course, they never had any intention of doing business in those locations in the first place.

December is usually a busy month for M&A. Everyone wants to close the books before year-end, and no one wants that more than me. So it was the middle of December one year, and every deal had closed but one. The laggard transaction was the sale of a public relations company to a global advertising concern. The buyer's lawyer was holding things up. I phoned the buyer to find out why and learned the buyer's attorney advised against taking over the seller's third-party payroll services contract, and the vendor wouldn't terminate the contract. I stirred the pot some more and found out the seller wanted to terminate the contract but couldn't because the payroll company's lawyer insisted on holding to the letter of the contract. So for about $160, the mental pipsqueaks held up a deal worth millions. The fees and billable hours generated to accommodate them probably reached five figures. The global ad company paid for the contract for the rest of the year. By that time I returned from Hawaii on January 1, the deal was done and the pipsqueaks were gone from my life. Happy New Year!

One time, I got a contract in the mail for a deal someone else did that needed reworking. I proceeded to go through it carefully. Most of the agreement made sense, but it contained two clauses that were baffling. As I was reading the paperwork, the phone rang—it was my new client's attorney. She said she had a couple of questions about two of the clauses.

"Funny, so do I," I told her.

"Maybe you could explain them," she said.

"Why would I do that?" I said. "You wrote them!"

She sighed. "I know, I know. Could you try to explain them anyway?"

The client ended up changing lawyers and is now living happily with revised, intelligible documents.

On one deal, I drafted a letter of intent and sent it to my client, the seller. The proposal was that the seller would leave about forty-five days of working capital in the company, worth about $2 million. My client sent it to the buyer, whose lawyer sent it back with markups. The working capital clause was marked up to say, "Excluding cash." Excluding cash? That means we would be leaving about $10 million extra for them. It would have been the stupidest agency deal in history.

The lawyer was very young, and I think this was the first deal she ever did—I wonder if she ever did another one. I deleted the markups and sent it back with a note: "Kindly call me."

She called, and I explained how working capital in deals is handled. I tried to do this politely. It seemed to work. Her client signed, and the deal closed.

Give a lawyer a copy of the Gettysburg Address and watch him or her mark it up! I don't think even the Ten Commandments would be safe.

I've often wondered why attorneys do some of the things they do. I get documents where they write, "You will pay [the firm, the buyer, the seller, whatever] 50 percent of $10,000." Sometimes I redline the percentage phrase, do the math, and insert the actual number—in this case, $5,000.

Lawyers hate when I do this. Once I sent back a contract where I deleted the percentage phrase, and the lawyer reprimanded me in an email. So I redlined the document and this time inserted my own arithmetical substitute: "25 percent of $20,000."

Needless to say, the humor was not appreciated. It was back to square one.

One time, a client sent me a lawyer's markup of my engagement letter. The altered document capped my hourly fees at $30,000. I called and asked him why. The client blamed the lawyer, which I hear all the time. I added "plus 10 percent" to the fee-cap clause and sent it back. The lawyer crossed out the phrase and returned the document. This time I didn't respond.

The next day, the client phoned and asked me about the contract.

"OK, fine," I said. "I'll sign it."

The client knew something was up. "What is it, David?"

"What do you mean?" I said innocently. "I said I'd sign it."

"I know you," he said. "You never give in like that. What's the deal?"

"No deal. When I hit the $30,000 cap, I'll just stop talking, even if I'm midsentence."

The client told me to reinsert the "plus 10 percent" and he'd ignore the lawyer's advice. Good decision.

Buyers' fees incurred postclosing are usually a big surprise to first-time sellers. Sellers like to focus on benefits like expected proceeds and multiples from the proposed sale; they tend to overlook the costs and "gotchas" that can reduce sales proceeds and shrivel profits. Buyers are certainly entitled to reasonable fees for providing services like insurance coverage, legal services, cybersecurity, human resource administration, audit and tax work, and more. The big question is, What's reasonable?

Buyers' lawyers like to slip in clauses that can dilute profit by many hundreds of thousands—sometimes millions—of dollars. In most industry deals, the buyer pays the seller a down payment based on a multiple of the firm's recent average profits and then pays the rest, the earnout, based on the level of the firm's profitability moving forward. Terms are structured over an agreed-upon number of years. If the seller's agency loses momentum and isn't as profitable postsale, the expected sales proceeds wither.

When this happens, the seller may claim that the buyer's fees are the problem and try to negotiate them down to restore profitability. Obviously, you want to arrive at terms that are fair to both sides at inception so that things move forward smoothly postsale. When both sides are reasonable, this is not difficult.

Some buyers come up with new schemes to clamp down profits. One of my favorites is "General Corporate Allocation Costs." Lawyers must stay up nights thinking these things up. The first time I spotted that in a contract, I challenged it immediately:

"What's this?" I asked.

"That is the General Corporate Allocation Cost clause," the lawyer said. "Is there a problem?"

"Yes, there's a problem. What the &^*! does it mean?"

"It means that under conditions that we can't prespecify, the buyer will in the course of conducting business perform certain activities that will potentially incur uncapped expenses, which will be billed by my client at a reasonable rate."

"Can you say that again?" I asked.

"No."

"I didn't think you could. It sounds to me that you're pushing my client to sign a contract that will oblige her to pay a fee that will be based on what your client feels like charging and that will be as high as your client likes. Our only recourse is to keep our fingers crossed your client forgets to bill."

"Well, I wouldn't say it exactly that way, but give or take, yes."

"You can say it any way you like; my client isn't signing. Let me ask, Does the term *unfair* mean anything to you?"

The concept of fair payment rates for services to be rendered by the buyer after the deal often surprises sellers. Sellers often don't consider that M&A deals should necessarily reflect in the transaction's structure the continuing relationship between the parties. The deals serve to establish terms for future delivery of business services going both ways.

Buyers are sometimes insulted when sellers charge them or their companies reasonable market rates, contending that they should be paying *less than* market rates since, after all, they're now all part of the same corporate family.

That might be nice, but that isn't how things equitably work.

I was about to close a sale transaction with a major holding company. I had asked the client early on, as I always do, "Do you have any outstanding litigation? Do you know of or have any prior incidents that could result in a litigation or a claim? Are there any tax or other audits or open investigations?"

The client said no to every question, so everything looked good.

The night before the scheduled closing, I got a phone call from the buyer's attorney, who told me we were not closing—they had just discovered fourteen complaints made against the seller's principal, my client. It turned out that when the guy was hiring, he would have breast-measurement contests among applicants. He had a small staff but apparently did extensive employment interviews—and measuring.

I called the client. "Is this true?" I asked.

"Yes," he said.

"Why didn't you tell me about the complaints?"

"I just forgot," he said.

The deal never closed. He deserved a double D.

Many lawyers are lovely people who make doing business a pleasure. I work all the time with Brad Schwartzberg, a partner at Davis & Gilbert LLP, which represents most of the major advertising holding companies. He called me up and said he was representing Dentsu, an advertising company that wanted to buy agencies that represent Toyota. He asked if I knew any agencies fitting that bill. It so happened that I did. Inside of three days, we had a letter of intent and began moving forward on an agreement. When people know what they want and know the rules of engagement, doing deals can be a piece of cake.

CHAPTER 17

I'M NOT YOUR TYPICAL ACCOUNTANT

The company accountant is shy and retiring. He's shy a quarter of a million dollars. That's why he's retiring.

—Milton Berle

Every client gets my best work. Some clients have been especially effusive in expressing their appreciation for my efforts.

A few months after joining Halpern, Goldstein & Company, I went on a business trip to Upstate New York with Goldstein. I had no suitcase, so I borrowed one, on my mother's insistence.

As for Goldstein, he brought his clothes and everything else in a paper bag. The paper bag was not even new; it had grease stains. It was during this trip that I realized that if you're so cheap, your checkbook groans when you tear out a check, clients won't trust you; they realize the lifelong cheapskate isn't a reliable source of financial advice. It's sad when people who hire you to help manage their finances dump you because you're so cheap. That's why you should never want to be hired because you charge lower rates than someone else. Today, if someone were to say to me, "You charge too much," I'd say, "Thank you."

Back on Court Street, it became obvious pretty quickly that I was not a shrinking violet waiting to be told what to do. In fact, the more the partners kept their distance from me, the happier I was. I did my work, went out to see clients, made the clients happy, and came back. The clients paid their bills, and Halpern and Goldstein were happy.

Meanwhile, I was champing at the bit. Clients who expected a Goldstein 2.0 or Halpern 2.0 were not ready for David Wiener. I came to the conclusion that my firm was undervaluing my services and notified my clients that I was adjusting my fees.

I wasn't able to bill more per month or by project, as the firm's rates were set by the partners, but I did adjust other things. Over the years, for no extra fees, Halpern and Goldstein jumped through hoops whenever clients asked—and even sometimes when they didn't. Clients had gotten so used to getting a lot of extras thrown in that they weren't extras anymore. I redrew the line: no more free extras. In some cases, I decided that we'd keep our hourly rates, only we'd clearly redefine what the scope of work was. When the scope was defined, the pay rate became a bit more equitable.

When they learned what I was doing, the partners were furious. I pointed out that almost no one had complained. As for our finances, the firm was bringing in much more money because of me—they liked that part.

When Halpern died and Goldstein made me a partner, things proceeded reasonably well, as long as contact between us was minimal. We argued over billing all the time. Goldstein's attitude—and Halpern's was the same—was that if you were too aggressive about adjusting fees and charges, the clients would defect. They were terrified of losing clients—heck, they were terrified of clients, period. I believe that being defensive leads to clients doubting your value. That's how professional services business relationships go bad.

Halpern and Goldstein set their fees when they got a new client and raised them once a century. The fee covered anything and everything, and no new or additional fees were ever charged. What started out, arguably, as fair value shriveled over time. Eventually a client had children, the children gained in-laws and grandchildren, and things like trust funds entered the picture. In some cases, we ended up handling the tax returns of clients' housekeepers and other household staff. There really was no end to it.

What's more, clients didn't appreciate it. They didn't really value the extra things we were doing for them because they just accrued.

After I was with the firm for a while, I started insisting on setting my own fees. I was clear with clients about which services this entailed. When clients wanted more, they had to pay more. I increased my fees periodically, as my own costs went up too. Today this approach is called scope billing. I didn't use the term at the time, but that was my philosophy.

After I left, I learned Goldstein had lowered his fees. I'm sure that in his mind, this was to make his firm, now that I was gone, more competitive. That was a mistake; it sent the message to his clients that with me gone, the firm's services were worth less. What a ridiculous thing to do.

Clients pick up on when you feel apologetic about your fees. I don't care if you're billing $100 an hour or $1,000, once you set your rates, you must be committed to them. If you don't believe you're worth what's printed on your invoices, your clients certainly won't.

Accountants who struggle financially really should analyze why that is. I see too many accountants who unfortunately see themselves as commodities. They may buy their wardrobe at places like Jos. A. Bank, but mentally, they're from the thrift shop. When they talk to people, they look at the person's shoes. Raise your eyes, my brethren. At least look at belt buckles.

The accounting profession has a bad reputation, continuously reinforced, of producing nerdy, insecure, socially immature practitioners—and some will say my assessment is overly kind. Accountants may think that interpersonal skills don't matter, that everything happens on the spread-sheet. They're flat-out wrong. How you deal with people matters a great deal.

I say this as someone who has tried, over many years, to master the social graces. It's no secret that I am not innately sociable, so I try harder. Sometimes I do need refresher courses. But I make a point of trying. I'm no Fred Astaire, but I've learned to fake dance. I know which fork to use for seafood and not to wear my napkin around my neck when I eat. If you invite me to a social function, I won't embarrass you.

One day, Steve Felsher, then CFO at Grey Global Group Inc., called me and asked when I'd be making my next trip to Cincinnati.

"Hopefully never," I said.

He ignored my wisecrack and asked if I could go see a small company Grey very much wanted to buy. What, I asked, did that have to do with me? It turned out something had happened at an earlier sit-down, and the principal was unwilling to meet again with them.

In other words, I was getting asked to be the wingman.

I said yes.

I got off the phone and called the proposed seller. I explained I was going to be in town—"never" turned out to be an exaggeration—and asked if he could spare ten minutes for me.

He agreed, although it was clear he could have thought of a hundred better things to do. I flew to Cincinnati, taxied to his company, and was promptly escorted into his office.

Mr. Hard-to-Get shook my hand, sat back down, and immediately looked at his watch. And I don't mean he looked at it discretely; he extended his left arm and looked intently into the face of his watch.

It was a tough conversation; he was not, to put it mildly, warm and fuzzy. I suspect he had never gotten around to reading Dale Carnegie's instructive book *How to Win Friends and Influence People*—which, by the way, I have.

My new friend was again examining his timepiece and was about to sound the one-minute warning when a bell rang in my head. His last name was unusual, and I had been trying to place it while chatting him up, however one-sided the conversation. It suddenly occurred to me that my wife's gynecologist had the same last name—turned out the gynecologist was his sister-in-law. He and I had a nice conversation about this little coincidence.

The ice melted, and my new friend agreed to a second meeting with Grey. A few moments later, I was out the door and on my way to the airport. The deal got done, the buyer and seller were both pleased, and I got a nice check from Grey.

I haven't been to Cincinnati since.

Today, I set my own rates. Because I believe it's about the value, not the price, I don't feel I have to lower my prices to compete. Earlier this year, I raised my hourly rate to $825. Sometimes someone will ask, "How do you have the nerve to charge $825?" My stock answer: "Because I don't yet have the nerve to charge $925."

I will in the near future. You can bet on it.

Unlike many accountants, I like to be paid when I do the work. I often include my bill when I mail back tax returns or other documents. You open the envelope, and out pops my bill on top of the completed work. Why not? There's a sign in the doctor's office saying it's customary for payments to be made when services are rendered. When you go to a barber, you pay him after he cuts your hair. Why not the same for accounting services?

I got a phone call from the CEO of a small Midwest agency inviting me to interview in person for a tax and accounting services job. He told me there were seventeen accounting firms coming to interview. I didn't like the sound of that, so I said to him, "I'll make it easier for you. Now you have sixteen firms to consider." He got annoyed. I never truly understood why.

What some other accountants do continues to amaze me after all these years. I once represented a big agency that engaged me to sell their business. I negotiated a 70 percent asset sale on an installment sale / earnout basis. Sometime later, a tax return was prepared by the agency's midwestern CPA firm. I asked to see a draft, so the client sent it via email.

Several minutes later, my client's CFO called and asked, "Are they OK?" Just by looking at the first page, I knew the answer was most assuredly no. The accountant had the client paying taxes on more than their gross proceeds. How can you pay taxes on more than your gross? The answer is you can't, unless somebody made grievous errors.

I do not recall if I said the last sentence aloud.

My client said good-bye, hung up, and called back an hour later.

"I looked at the returns," he said, taking my advice to look over the documents. "I see the problem."

"Which is what?" I asked.

"They omitted a $10 million deduction."

"That's part of the problem, sure," I said. "But not all of it."

I suggested he get the tax preparer on the phone for a three-way conversation. What an interesting experience it was to hear someone casually justify overlooking a $10 million deduction without a word of apology or a mention of the far more significant screw-ups in the reporting of the sales proceeds. It was like listening to someone describe losing a borrowed ballpoint pen.

What he lost was the client, who retained us to prepare the returns and those for the subsequent years.

I was preparing a client for a sale one December when I met with the agency's accountant. We were going over their financials, and I saw that their year-end bank deposits had dried up.

"It seems like you have a billing problem," I said.

"No," the client's accountant said. "We just hold the end-of-year checks and deposit them right after January 1. I lower the client's tax bite for the year." He lowered his voice and smiled. "The client thinks I'm brilliant."

I've seen cats with that same look after swallowing the canary.

"So it's tax planning, huh?" I said.

The accountant nodded.

"OK, so you're holding checks from, say, twenty-five clients dated this year, and then January 2, you deposit them all. Think the IRS might just happen to notice that?"

"Sir, I've never been audited by the IRS," he said. "It's outrageous of you to suggest that!"

"So if you never have a colonoscopy, you can never get colon cancer?"

I admit I can get a little sarcastic at times, especially when confronted with abject stupidity—and illegality.

One time, the CEO of an ad agency called me in and told me that he was thinking of selling the agency and asked if I would represent them. We talked a while, and he agreed to open their books; I wanted to see what the company was doing before I agreed to anything.

I was glad I did. The company was not making money and had severe cash-flow problems, but they had plenty of "investments" on the books. The investments were a series of new-business pitches that each cost between $50,000 and $100,000.

"I'm sure any prospective buyer is going to wonder, much as I am now, what new business came in from these investments," I said politely.

"Oh," he said. "None, actually."

"You mean, you pitched the business and lost? Every time?"

"Yes," he answered. "We didn't get any of those clients."

Now, this happens frequently. Even the top hot agencies don't win every pitch. On the other hand, top agencies don't claim their failed pitches are investments and keep them on their books; they are considered sunk costs.

I pointed that out.

He said, "I appreciate your opinion"—opinion?—"but I happen to know for a fact that we can leave these investments on the books. You should appreciate that, because it raises the value of our company. So do you want to represent us?"

Thank you very much, but no.

Note that a few months later, when they were about to go out of business, I was retained and sold the agency for an amount that allowed them to pay off their debts. The principals even kept their reputations intact and got good positions and successful careers elsewhere. And in the end, they did write off their "investments." I assume their accountant is continuing to practice his value-enhancing methods.

Another time, a small media-buying company called me in and told me they were thinking about putting their agency on the block. I met with the two partners and their accountant. The accountant had an interesting routine he worked on them: he'd do the company's forecasted financial statements, and whatever profit they made, the company would write him a check for that amount at the very end of the year and take an income tax deduction, thus eliminating their taxable profit.

For example, let's say their profit was $3 million. The accountant wouldn't deposit the check until early the following year so he did not have to pick up the corresponding income. This way the company eliminated their profit, and the accountant would give them the same amount back at the end of the following year, interest-free. So when they got to the end of the next year and now the company was forecasted to make a $4 million profit, they would send the accountant a check for $7 million (the $3 million from the prior year plus $4 million from the current year) to wipe out their profits for this year and the prior year, and the whole cycle would start all over again. The accountant had the use of their money, interest-free, and portrayed himself as a genius.

I told them that this was clearly tax fraud and advised them to stop immediately. Both partners scrunched their faces into scowls. I figured maybe these guys were just very naïve, so I asked, "What's the matter?"

One of the partners said, "You're not being very nice to our accountant. He's been an incredible help to us for many years. You owe him an apology."

I stood up, walked out, and threw my notes in the garbage.

They retained me a few weeks later to help them sell their agency to a buyer who recommended me. The deal closed, and they ceased their antics.

CHAPTER 18

THE VIRTUOUS CIRCLE

Draw a circle and bisect it. Bisect it again. Put the words "Great Work" in one segment, "Great People" in the second, "Great Clients" in the third, and "Great Profits" in the forth. Each segment is separate, but all four are necessary for the circle to be complete.

The concept is simple, but the execution is always challenging. To produce great work, you need great people on board. Great people will attract great clients. A roster of great clients will produce great profits. The profits are needed to pay the great people to do the great work, and so on.

This is the Virtuous Circle. When all four components work in sync, the company is successful. People enjoy coming to work. The phones ring with good news. Prospects start calling you. Life is good. The tough part is making the decisions that keep the circle intact.

Consider the owner of a certain ad agency. He loved the idea of the Virtuous Circle, provided it applied to someone else—he was sure it didn't apply to him. He treated his business like a cash cow, cashing profits to finance his luxurious lifestyle. "Lighten up," he'd tell anyone who questioned his style. "It's my business. Who am I hurting?"

In fact, he was hurting his business. He lived lavishly, with a beautiful second home, first-class travel, late-model fancy cars, the works. Nothing was too good. It was top shelf all the way.

At restaurants, he always picked up the check.

He'd say, "Why not? My business is doing well. I can afford it."

The problem was that he confused revenue with profit. He was certainly entitled to take a profit, but he was greedy, in that he took far too much profit for himself, and shortsighted, in that he shortchanged his agency, which needed the investment much more than he needed the continuous flow of goodies that he so generously bestowed on himself.

He skimped on the salaries of his employees. In the ad business, we always say that your most important assets walk out the door every night, but if you pay them too little, they may never walk back in the next day!

He continued to treat himself generously yet refused to hire a superior creative director, which his agency desperately needed. He wouldn't pay the rates that the top talent can get elsewhere. Now with a mediocre staff, the agency couldn't pull the big accounts from the big companies. Customer-side execs certainly know the market; they know quality when they see it just as surely as they know mediocrity when they see that. They smiled politely at this agency's pitch sessions but would end up going with different agencies. The agency owner in question, meanwhile, blamed his prospects and landed just enough projects from big companies and accounts of record from second-rate smaller companies to stay in the black and foster the illusion that the company was doing well.

Those second-rate smaller companies are never interested in cutting-edge, award-winning work. Why? That would push them out of their comfort zone. They want same old, same old. Of course they *tell* their account execs they want their spots to stand out, but they would never approve anything different than a less edgy version of the clichéd spot they did last year. Their budget? As you'd expect, it's miniscule. These clients will always take small-market spots when even the local insomniacs have turned their sets off. As far as production quality goes, they're all for it. Why, the boss's son is an aspiring actor and would be delighted to appear in the commercial at nonequity rates; it will be his first screen credit. As for print, stock art is fine. Tell the art director to go with the generic stuff that doesn't carry licensing fees. And so on.

What kind of work comes out of accounts like those? You know the answer: mediocre. The way the agency owner ran his company, the Virtuous Circle became a Vicious Circle. But is it possible to turn things around?

Absolutely. But it takes financial discipline, and a lot of it. If you find yourself in a similar situation as the agency owner, you need to do the following:

Close the books each month. Keep your receivables under thirty days by billing promptly.

Track your client pipeline. Code each prospect by estimated size of account. Invest most of your resources into winning the biggest of those accounts. Your business development head should know where each prospect is at a given point and be able to estimate when the prospect will become a client. If your business development person can't do that accurately, you need a new person. Speaking of . . .

Hire the best people. Look to hire people younger, smarter, more talented in certain key areas, and hungrier than you. You don't need more people like you; you need people better than you.

Pay them well. Introduce a bonus system. Do your research—or task someone to do it for you—and find out how the most generous bonus system in your market works. Then match or exceed its structure.

Virtually any agency that becomes best of breed grows beyond the talents of its founders. Ralph Ammirati and Martin Puris are great examples. Both are talented creatives. During the life of their agency, they hired and held on to competent people to run their financial, legal, and business departments. The partners themselves anchored a changing cast of art directors, copywriters, and more who complemented their skills rather than duplicated them. They encouraged their people to develop their careers, were supportive of them, and brought in talented new people at every opportunity. When the time came to sell their agency, they sold it at an optimal rate.

Ammirati & Puris personified the Virtuous Circle. They ran one of the greatest creative agencies that ever opened its doors. What a pleasure it was to work with them. They deserved every ounce of their considerable success.

CHAPTER 19

HOW TO STOP AD EXECS FROM BANGING THE BACK OF YOUR CHAIR AT THE FOUR SEASONS

In 2005, I was at the Four Seasons Hotel's restaurant in New York with my family enjoying a birthday celebration dinner. Or I was trying to enjoy dinner, as a guy at the table behind me kept banging into my chair. I moved my chair closer to my table, but he did not stop.

About halfway through my steak, he banged into me with enough force to bring down any of the Giants' running backs. I swiveled around, faced the back of the offending chair, and said at the top of my voice, "Am I in your freaking way?" Only I didn't say *freaking*.

The man turned around and said, "David?" It was Chuck Porter, whose agency, Crispin Porter + Bogusky, I had helped sell a few months before.

We had never met in person, but he recognized my voice. We shook hands, and I introduced my family.

Afterward, Sheila said to me, "I bet you wished you hadn't said that."

"No, I'm glad I did," I said. "Notice he stopped banging into me?"

I've seen so many successful parents spoil their children by solving their problems for them. Kids who never have the experience of dealing with adversarial issues never learn how to make their own decisions and deal with the real world. People who had to struggle to achieve success often try to make it easier for their kids, bringing them into the business and giving them real responsibilities before they've demonstrated any ability to handle them. Kids realize this and never develop the self-esteem that comes from creating your own success in life. You can inherit a job and a company, but you can't inherit self-esteem or self-confidence.

I've held to this principle when it comes to helping my own kids, with one exception. I did make a phone call to a client on behalf of one of my daughters, who was looking for her first job after college (she got it). She is smart and hardworking—this is my completely objective opinion, of course—and I think she would have gotten the job anyway.

Our youngest daughter, Laura, worked in advertising before she gave birth to Alexis. Entirely on her own, she got her second job with Donny Deutsch's agency, where she was known by her married name. I went in to see Donny one time and of course stopped to say hello to her. We hugged, and I gave her a kiss on the cheek. Donny happened to pass by at that moment, and his jaw dropped. I then introduced his employee as my daughter; she had never mentioned it. Surprise, Donny.

The advertising industry is, like most glamorous media industries, a hotbed of nepotism. People hire their relatives all the time—sons, daughters, nieces, nephews, aunts, uncles, brothers, sisters-in-law, third cousins once removed. I realize that family members can be employees and that doesn't necessarily compromise their output or make them any less professional or qualified. But it does, however, raise a big yellow flag in the form of independent choice, specifically whether agency employees are truly free to make creative choices when those choices involve the owners' family members.

Here's an example. The creative director wants to take a new approach to a client. He is determined to try something a little different, maybe a little edgy. He has a photographer in mind he'd like to engage but feels uneasy bypassing the owner's daughter (or son, or fill in the blank), who does much of the agency's photography. He ends up using the owner's relation, who is an excellent photographer but not the best person for the job.

When I mention this scenario to the owner, he invariably thrusts his hands to the ceiling, palms out, and says, "David, David, where do you come up with these ideas? Everybody here knows they can work with whomever they want. There's absolutely no pressure to use [fill in the name] who just happens to be my [fill in the family connection]."

OK. I get it. But when I talk with staff members, they usually don't sound like they got that memo.

My general advice to owners is, let Junior find jobs on his own. When family members get their skills up to speed, you can hire them. Otherwise, you're painting targets on their backs, as everyone will believe, justified or not, that they were hired because they're your kin. Why do that to them?

On rare occasions, an antinepotism policy works to an agency's disadvantage, especially after the reputation and ability of the relative have independently been established. Jay Chiat's son, Marc, was an accomplished director, and Ralph Ammirati's son, Robert, was an accomplished photographer. Chiat/Day often used Robert and Ammirati & Puris used Marc, but their fathers' agencies never took advantage of their respective sons' gifts.

A tradesman overcharged me the other day. I know approximate prices for small business and household services, and I know I had been overcharged. Nevertheless, I paid the bill. The guy probably thought he had put one over on me—he hadn't. He made a few extra bucks on the transaction, but I got something much more valuable: the knowledge that I'll never hire him again. Believe me, I'll find a way to let people know, and it won't be on social media.

A woman who lives in our community visited the other night with her husband. She's Jewish. One of his hobbies is that he's part of a group that does reenactments of Luftwaffe battles in costume (uniform). I wonder what they talk about at night.

We're becoming ruder and ruder as a society. After a workout at the Friars Club gym recently, I sat down on a bench in the locker room. CNN was on, so I started watching—and not out of the corner of my eye, either; I stared at the screen no more than ten feet away. Barely a minute later, a guy stepped in front of me and changed the channel—he didn't even look at me.

What did he put on? Cartoons. It was obvious he couldn't care less about being rude. Some cartoon animal or another was hitting another cartoon animal over the head and making a racket at top volume. Using the plumiest voice this side of Eton, I said, "So are these good cartoons?"

"I should think so," the moron said. "I wrote them."

"Listen," I said, "everyone's entitled to their time on the learning curve."

Quite a few people I meet in the course of doing deals become good friends, even though we may not speak or meet often, but when we do, it's always enjoyable. Richard Kirshenbaum always calls before the Jewish holidays, often to share a memory of something his late father said that seems appropriate for the moment. After we sold Kirshenbaum Bond & Partners, Richard invited Sheila, me, and Jon and Rebecca Bond to dinner with him and his wife, Dana. At the dinner, he said he valued my dedication, appreciated the deal I did for them, and other lovely things. Then he presented me with a gold Cartier watch, with the following inscribed on the back: "In Gratitude. Richard & Jon."

I do a lot of business in restaurants. It's not just that I enjoy eating out, which I do, but I learn a great deal by observing how people handle themselves. What do they order to drink? Do they treat the server with respect? Do they grab the check or sit back and watch me take it? Do they tip 10 percent if no one's watching? The things you learn by going to lunch!

I admit, sometimes I'm jealous of Sheila. In my next life, I'm coming back as her.

Richard Kirshenbaum, like me, has been happily married for many years now. He has a great expression that I often use: "I married my third wife first." I love it!

CHAPTER 20

MEETING BILL RUSSELL AND OTHER BIG NAMES

About sixteen years ago, a client introduced me to professional basketball player Bill Russell. Bill has been called the foremost athlete of the twentieth century, and deservedly so. His intellectual capabilities, his ferocious competitive instincts, and his compelling leadership qualities—apart from his nonpareil athletic skills—were integral to his game. These are qualities that matter enormously in life and in business as well as in sports. These characteristics and the personalities associated with them endure much longer than the numbers that flash on scoreboards.

Bill Russell was born at a time when discrimination and inequality massively restricted the lives of black people. To achieve equality, Bill had to work harder, develop his skills faster, and out-compete everyone he encountered. He became the leader his teams needed to triumph, winning their respect by his conduct as well as his skills. His athletic achievements began in his brain; his extraordinary coordination and the athletic accomplishments came second. His message was to use your talent and ignore people trying to make life difficult for you. Decades into his retirement, Bill still conducts himself like the champ he is.

When Bill and I were introduced, we talked about working together on a project to help an athlete repair his image. Although nothing came from those discussions, Bill and I became friendly. He later invited me to play at Don Imus's Celebrity Charity Golf Tournament as part of his foursome. The group was Bill, a public relations guy from the Boston Celtics, professional golfer Chris DiMarco, and me.

We arranged to meet at an exclusive and, shall we say, highly selective golf club in New Jersey. I called Bill and jokingly asked him how I'd find him at the club. I learned quickly that Bill is a man who knows a setup when he hears one:

"David, I'll be one of the very few six-foot, ten-inch black men there," he replied. He was indeed right.

At the first tee, he said that since we'd be spending a good bit of time together, he wanted me to think of him as Bill Russell the man, not Bill Russell the basketball star. He teed up and swung. After he shanked the ball thirty feet due east, it was my turn for a punchline: "Well, I sure as #*/%! won't think of you as Bill Russell the golfer!"

He burst out laughing.

On another occasion, we got together and played a casual round of golf at the Metedeconk National Golf Club, a club I belong to. This was a club-run member/guest tournament. Bill and I played with two of my friends in a foursome. The camaraderie was great. The golf itself was unexceptional save for the remarkable experience of competing along-side one of the greatest athletes in history. On the eighteenth green, the match came down to my sinking a long putt. I admit I was nervous.

Bill sensed this and whispered, "Bet you never thought you'd be play-ing with an Olympic athlete who would be depending on you to come through."

I looked up at him, but rather than feeling more pressure, I relaxed. Maybe I just wanted to show Bill Russell the stuff I was made of. With a tremble I hoped wasn't noticeable, I putted. The ball sank a few moments later, and the great Bill Russell bent over laughing. He didn't stop guf-fawing for two minutes straight. They say great athletes perform at their best under pressure—but I think a little of Bill's grace had rubbed off on me. I wish I could bottle it.

In 2002, Bill published a book about leadership titled *Russell Rules: 11 Lessons on Leadership from the Twentieth Century's Greatest Winner.* The century had just ended, but I thought the book was nevertheless motiva-tional and inspiring. Some months later, our mutual friend asked if I had any ideas to help him sell some books and maybe get on the best-seller list. I suggested I'd help if Bill would come to my favorite restaurant in New Jersey—Anjelica's in Sea Bright—and sign a few copies of *Russell Rules*.

I turned the event into a fund raiser for the Benjamin Wiener Foundation. Sheila and I had established this nonprofit years earlier in memory of my late father to help people stricken with cancer pay for the costs of treatment and treatment-related daily living expenses.

Bill quickly agreed. We scheduled a day, and I invited quite a few of my friends and colleagues. I bought 350 copies of *Russell Rules*, and Bill signed them, inscribed the books for those in attendance, and spoke movingly about his book and the current state of the NBA—he even mentioned my winning putt. We sold the signed copies for the benefit of the foundation for $350 each. Additionally, Bill donated three autographed basketballs. I was told by Bill to sell two and keep one for myself, which I still have. So far, however, none of his basketball skills have rubbed off on me. I guess any athletic luck he lent me was limited to the links that one day.

Years later, when Bill stayed at my home, he saw the signed ball. He asked why I kept it—he knew that I'm not a basketball fan. I told him that I couldn't sell it yet—it will be worth much more when he's dead. He laughed loudly.

The most baffling individual I've ever worked for is another Bill—Bill Murray. Whatever words you come up with to describe him—actor, comedian, performer—seem inadequate and off mark. Bill does not use an agent; he has an 800 phone number and will call you back if and when he chooses to. I see someone has taken on the challenge of explaining Murray's perplexing nature in a book called *The Tao of Bill Murray*. I have read it. To paraphrase the old skit from *Saturday Night Live*, his old stomping grounds, he's Bill Murray, and we're not.

I met Carl Reiner, Mel Brooks, and Tony Randall in the fall of 1991 while cochairing, along with the late Saul Waring, the annual benefit dinner for the Weizmann Institute of Science in Israel. Having spent formative summers as a junior wannabe *tummler* in the Catskills, when I realized I would be cochairing a show with these guys, I felt like I must have died and gone to Borscht Belt heaven.

My connection to the Weizmann Institute was through Saul. Like many ad execs, Saul was often called on to do pro bono work for good causes. He helped raise millions of dollars over the years by lending his creative skills, his marketing know-how, and his connections with the entertainment industry to serve a variety of causes.

For the Weizmann Institute benefit dinner, Saul was intent on creating a lively, genuinely entertaining event rather than duplicating the usual kosher rubber-chicken fare. The typical gala entertainment is well meaning but gets tired fast; you might not die of old age before they get through the introductions, but you sure as hell might nod off.

Along with bringing me on as his cochair, Saul also got his friend Bill Persky, the brilliant comedy writer whose credits include *The Dick Van Dyke Show* and *Kate & Allie*, to write the script. Bill assured us he

Charitable work has been a very rewarding part of my life. The Weizmann Institute of Science in Israel presented me with this vase in recognition of my leadership and fundraising work for their organization.

Not all of Frank Gehry's building designs are equally celebrated. Gehry's Chiat/Day Binoculars Building is iconic, but the restaurant concept that he designed for a Jay Chiat pet project was a notable misstep.

would keep the introductions, official business, and other verbal "paper-work" to a minimum so our guest stars could shine. Bill proceeded to do just that. He wrote a few great bits, which our superlative cast performed magnificently.

When you're presenting talent like Mel Brooks, Carl Reiner, and Tony Randall, writing skits for them is like showing Mickey Mantle how to hit a baseball. We sat back and watched as Randall took over the stage and did what he did so well. Michael Douglas, who stood in for his father, Kirk, as the evening's honoree, was charming, funny, and gracious. The inimitable Mel Brooks and Carl Reiner revived a few choice riffs from their legendary 2,000-Year-Old-Man routine. They killed it. Laughter, laughter, applause, applause. Afterward, a swinging jazz band played, and well-heeled rug-cutters filled the floor.

Note that all the talent volunteered their services.

I was surprised and a little saddened afterward to learn that despite the rousing applause and successful fund-raising, not everyone appreciated our efforts. For reasons I never officially learned, we were not asked to cochair ever again. I heard through third parties that it was considered too "lowbrow." I still support the institute by buying tickets to their gala every year and in many other ways, and all these years later, I still hear from people who have never forgotten that night.

The next year, the dinner returned to the traditional route: the entertainment was provided by children of the scientists from the institute in Israel playing classical music, and the hour-long, humorless introductions were reinstated.

As mentioned earlier in the book, I met the famous architect Frank Gehry through Jay Chiat. Jay was a big admirer and personal friend of Gehry and hired him in the eighties to design Chiat/Day's Venice, Los Angeles, headquarters. Frank's design incorporated the specially commissioned "Giant Binoculars" sculpture by Claes Oldenburg. The structure itself would become known as the Binoculars Building. Gehry worked on it for more than a decade, completing it in 2001. Complications arose during the construction process when hazardous materials were discovered underground on the building site. This took place in the public eye, as the building was, not surprisingly, a magnet for public attention.

Jay was eager to have Frank finally finish the space so he could move in; he had been stuck in temporary Gehry-designed warehouse space—though everyone learned to love that office. When they finally did move in, the company had grown so much that space was tight. Still, Jay fell in love with the Binoculars Building for many reasons.

One reason was the open floor design. This was Jay's pet idea and worked very well in the new building. Jay felt people got too comfortable in private spaces to be creative, collaborative, and edgy. The open plan was far more space efficient, and people thrived on the creative noise, sound, and energy.

It looked clean too, as there was minimal space for clutter, though that didn't mean people were necessarily neat. Jay still used to sweep through the office, knocking clutter off desks. People didn't like this habit, as you can imagine.

Jay also bought some of Frank's designed furniture for his Manhattan office at 79 Fifth Avenue, including several unique corrugated-cardboard chairs and sofas. Jay also gravitated to Frank's wooden furniture, which he bought for the warehouse in Venice and for his own homes. When Chiat/Day moved downtown to Maiden Lane, the new office space didn't allow for the corrugated chairs, so he gifted one to me. It was the one I used to sit on in his office across from his desk. The cardboard chair is still in my great room and is a perennial conversation piece. It even survived Hurricane Sandy with only a few minor water stains.

When Chiat/Day moved their New York office from Fifth Avenue to Maiden Lane, Jay's open floor sensibilities morphed into "hoteling," which involved assigning people different work spaces based on day-to-day needs. Employees had lockers, unwired phones, and computer network plug-ins, and he left them to their own devices. Today, people work remotely all the time, settling into booths or pods in places like Starbucks and using smartphones in place of desktops or laptops. In this as well as so many things, Jay was ahead of his time.

Today, Google occupies the Binoculars Building. Whenever I see it, it reminds me of Frank, a very personable and accomplished man who enjoys challenging himself and doing the unexpected.

Some of the people I've met throughout my career could have stepped out of a Damon Runyon novel. As a young man, I had a circle

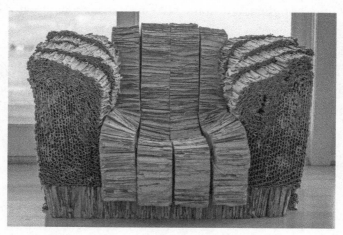

This Frank Gehry chair was originally in Jay Chiat's office. Jay later gifted it to me.

of clients—manufacturers, printers, factors, and so on—who met most Monday nights for dinner at places like Peter Luger, Marty's, and Sparks. I often joined them for business development and bonding purposes.

I was by far the youngest and likely the poorest of the group. Other people would join us as well. I remember Al Goldstein, the pornographer, coming around, although I never really spoke much with him.

As you can imagine, we ran up some hefty bills. We took turns picking up the tab. It was bad form to suggest it was someone else's night to pay and far worse to blow off the bill when it was your turn.

One night, when we got the bill, the whole table fell silent, waiting for someone to pick up the check—it was Mr. X's turn to pay. Who was X, you might ask? I didn't know; I had never asked what his real name was. You wouldn't have either, trust me.

Everyone looked at X. He turned to me and said calmly, "David? It's your turn to pay."

"Actually," I said even more calmly, "it's your turn."

Another person at the table said, "David's a CPA. He should know, right?"

Everyone nodded.

X took out his wallet and said, "I am so sorry. I only have this." He pulled out a crisp thousand-dollar bill—now that's something you don't see every day.

I paid.

The next week, I came prepared and stuffed my wallet with Andrew Jacksons and Ulysses S. Grants. At dinner, X went through the same routine when the check arrived: he pulled out the thousand-dollar bill, crisp as ever. I suspect this was the only use it got.

"No problem," I said, pulling out my wallet. "I have change."

After that night, X never joined us again.

CHAPTER 21

PEOPLE ARE IRRATIONAL

People are irrational about many things. One of the worst is pricing, and our human vulnerability to suggestion makes this even worse. Vendors selling multiple items priced at round numbers exemplify this irrationality. For example, supermarkets may price four oranges at $6. If you hang around the orange bin long enough, you'll see shoppers pick out exactly four oranges, put them in their baskets, and move on. If the supermarket instead advertised "$1.50 each"—which is the same thing—people would take fewer oranges.

Merchants of course know this. Economists call this demand-side pricing stimulation, a fancy way of saying people fill their shopping baskets when they think they're getting a bargain, even though they're not.

It's not limited to supermarkets. My neighborhood cigar store charges $100 for twenty cigars, always shown as on sale. Maybe cigars normally cost $6, but if you take their suggestion and buy them in bulk, you think you're getting a discount. I tested this once and brought nineteen to the register.

The clerk rang me up. "That will be $95, sir."

"Wait," I said. "I think I'll take one more." I grabbed an extra cigar and handed it to him. "Now how much?"

The clerk added the price to the total. "That will be $100, sir."

"So there really is no sale discount, is there?" I asked.

They smile at me less when I go in now. I live with that—but I also buy as many or as few cigars as I like.

I did some forensic work once for a client's girlfriend who was in the process of getting a divorce. Her future ex-husband's main asset was his medical practice, for which she wanted a valuation and analysis of profit and cash flow. She fully expected her former beloved would poor-mouth his cash flow when it came time to valuing his assets. I believe she expected that I would uncover hidden money or other evidence of fraud, anything to help bolster her negotiating position.

This medical practice specialized in terminating the pregnancies of mostly poor women—it was an abortion clinic. When I went in to look at their books, I took along my sister, Ruth, who worked for me at the time, to quell any of the staff's suspicions. It didn't seem to help. I sat down with the books in an overheated little room. About fifteen minutes later, two staffers burst in and loudly accused me of peeking into one of the treatment rooms. I can't imagine anyone sane looking at women getting abortions for kicks.

They threatened to call the cops. My sister assured them she'd been with me since we arrived and that I hadn't taken my nose out of the ledgers, which was true. As soon as they left, we started searching the room for a "second set" of books. How did I know there was a bogus second set? Instinct. Whenever someone accuses me of something illegal, unethical, or simply vile, I assume they're up to their eyeballs in much worse. They can't resist trying to tar me with the same brush they surely have handy.

We found the second set of books almost instantly, sitting in another drawer in another desk in the room. I opened the drawer and looked at the ledgers. There were lists of receipts for the same day in each book. One said about $3,000 with the listed items, and the other book listed the same items plus thousands more. The books looked identical from the outside. We made copies of both books, selecting different days as samples.

When the duplicitous physician was presented with proof of his bookkeeping scam, he quickly agreed to a settlement with his soon-to-be ex-wife. I needed a shower after the whole experience—and I used an awful lot of soap.

Saul Waring got into Siddha Yoga at one point through the woman he was seeing at the time. He believed in the power of chanting, and like a true convert, he tried to get his friends involved. He meant well, but there was little receptivity. One day, he invited us all to come to a lecture at a hotel in Manhattan for an hour or so. We all loved Saul, so we showed up on schedule. To say it inspired laughter is to say Babe Ruth hit a few home runs. It was OK until the chanting began. We chanted "Om Namah Shivaya, Om Namah Shivaya" over and over. "Om Namah Shivaya, Om Namah Shivaya," I chanted as I thought to myself, *What the hell am I doing here?* "Om Namah Shivaya." I nearly strained my groin trying not to laugh. I remember Dan Lufkin—founder of Donaldson, Lufkin & Jenrette—literally on the floor laughing. He quietly sneaked out a little later. When it was over, Sheila and I left quickly, managing to avoid any eye contact that might have elicited further invitations. None were extended, thankfully.

The other day, I realized I hadn't physically been to a closing in a very long time. It used to be that you'd wrap up a work session and say, "See you at closing." Not anymore. Today you handle any loose ends using PDFs and emails and close electronically. The buyer wires the seller the money—it takes ten or fifteen minutes. Things move fast. You don't have people grandstanding and giving little speeches to show how tough they are. You look at your bank account online and see the deposit. Done! I like it this way.

I eat out a lot. I'm lactose intolerant, and I'll occasionally order a pizza with no cheese. They often charge me an additional $3 or $4. I don't get that. How can you charge me more when it costs you less to make the product? I argued this vehemently with my local pizzeria. They refused to concede my point. The next time I went in, though, I saw they had dropped the surcharge. No explanation was given or asked for.

Jeff Weiss is a client and a dear friend. He does wonderful charity work and donates his time and money to people and never looks for anything in return. Some years ago, he invited Sheila and me to a three-week stay with him and his wife at a Pritikin Longevity Center in Pennsylvania. Pritikin is a strict and disciplined diet, exercise, and weight-loss center. He had claimed that he had free days to offer to his friends, as he was writing a book on the program.

When Sheila and I got to the hotel, they had no knowledge of Jeff Weiss. In fact, they gave me a refund check for $800 because he overpaid.

I immediately called Jeff, who admitted the ruse but said it was for a good cause—it was to help Sheila and me lose weight, eat healthier, and exercise. He pleaded with us to stay and complete the program. We did. We ended up shedding a few pounds, learned a bit about nutrition, and got into an exercise program. Sometimes other people can get you to do things for yourself you wouldn't do otherwise. And no, I did not keep the $800.

A client of mine was being audited and had selected his longtime CPA and former high school classmate to handle it. The CPA asked my client for $10,000 in cash, which he said would be used to pay the Internal Revenue Service agent conducting the audit. Obviously this was not legitimate. I told my client the CPA was full of crap, but he didn't want to make waves or accuse his old friend. When the audit's results were adverse, my client called and asked me to get involved. The first thing I did was ask the CPA to return the $10,000. I was offered half of it back. I told the CPA that if he didn't give me the full amount of money, I'd bring the matter up with the IRS's regional director. The CPA quickly paid the money, my client retained me instead, and I reworked the audit. The client and I became fast friends. It's nice when things work out right.

Jay Chiat once gifted me a fire-engine-red plank. It was about two inches thick, two feet wide, and fifteen feet long.

I looked it over. "What is it?"

"It's a piece of art, dummy," he said.

"What am I supposed to do with it?"

"You can display it at home. Red's a lucky color to the Chinese. John McCracken is the artist."

I thanked him and had the piece shipped home. I leaned it against the wall near the front door of my home. It proved to be a conversation piece and was the start of my small collection of mostly contemporary art. Some years later, a gallery owner visited my home and told me it was actually of substantial value. I couldn't control my instincts and sold it for about $65,000. Sheila and I used the money to open college savings accounts for our grandchildren.

CHAPTER 22

FIGHT, FLEE—OR LAUGH

In prehistoric times, mankind often had only two choices in crisis situations: fight or flee. In modern times, humor offers us a third alternative; fight, flee—or laugh.

—Robert Orben

During the early years of my career, I was constantly frustrated that the pace of change was much too slow. By "change," I mean acceptance for the things I wanted to do, which were in some cases a little different than what had always been done. The way things were always done sometimes seemed damn foolish to me. I thought I had better ideas—for example, sending bills promptly, automating what you can, paying people more to get the best work, working hard—but my ideas weren't always taken seriously.

In fact, they rarely were taken seriously.

People often blocked my suggestions or weren't receptive to my initiatives or recommendations. Some probably felt I was this brassy kid with big ideas who wasn't very respectful of his elders. Come to think of it, they were right. Some people turn on the charm under those circumstances, but as a partner once said of me, I must have failed charm school. I told him to go #@%^& himself.

My adversaries liked to trot out their arguments against me in public. They often didn't understand what I was suggesting and rephrased what I had in mind in ways that made me look foolish. They knew how to get my goat and enjoyed baiting the young know-it-all. I ended up snapping at them a lot, and that of course made things worse.

This really bugged me. I felt my life was plagued by stupid people—they seemed to pop up like mushrooms after a good rain.

Early on, Jay Chiat witnessed a pretty noisy exchange between me and one of the mushroom people. I don't remember what the argument was about anymore, nor does it matter. What I do remember is the advice I got, for which I'm grateful to this day:

Jay said, "David, you don't have to argue every point with these jerks. You're smarter than they are. Don't let them drag you down to their level."

"Great idea," I said. "How do I do that?"

"Instead of arguing, banter with them. Kid them. Someone argues with you, turn their position into a joke. Do it with a smile, a dollop of sarcasm they'll never pick up. They'll miss the joke, but everyone else will get it. Then bingo, you win."

"How do I win?"

He explained that when the other guy gets laughed at, you automatically win the argument. It's human nature. I was beginning to warm to this idea but didn't want to show my hand too quickly. Eventually, I saw that this was how Jay himself operated, at least some of the time.

"Watch your favorite comedians more closely," Jay went on. "Watch how they work the audience. Watch how they let people in on the joke. People will flock to the winner's side."

I put his advice to work almost immediately. I remember a client's staff accountant who always seemed to take particular pleasure in blocking everything I tried to do. No matter how stupid his comments were, I always took the bait.

Except now I was ready for him.

I remember being seated at the big conference table at my client's office. The CEO, the CFO, and most of the firm's senior managers were there, including my adversary, whom I'll call Bill (which is not his real name).

I had been asked to make a presentation on financing alternatives. I was about two minutes into my comments when he spoke out: "David," he interrupted, "you can't be serious. I explained last time that blah blah blah."

I let him finish his sentence.

"Great idea, Bill," I said. I added pleasantly, "So glad you figured this out. Let's keep doing what you've been doing, and it will be better tomorrow."

I smiled at him—I never did that. Bill looked at me suspiciously, knowing something was up. The others watched with interest. When he made a particularly dumb point, I jumped.

"Problem solved!" I said, smiling broadly. "We can go home early now!"

My comeback got a few laughs—probably because no one expected humor of any kind from grouchy me. It worked. Like any bully, Bill crumpled when I stood up for myself.

As time went on, I found myself increasingly attuned to how smart people use humor effectively. I became a big fan of people like Groucho Marx, Richard Pryor, George Carlin, Mel Brooks, Henny Youngman, Buddy Hackett, Don Rickles, and Milton Berle. I started reading books about them and by them, especially biographies and memoirs. The more I read, the more I felt I had in common with them. Many great comedians are Jews born in New York City. They survived on the humor their brains produced and their ability to convince other people they were right; it wasn't a stretch for me to identify with them.

I wasn't the only one either; advertising executives are often big fans of stand-up comics. In fact, Martin Puris was a stand-up comedian in his youth. A lot of my clients also shared my comedy "habit." Back a few years ago, comedy clubs became all the rage, and I used to get invitations to join clients when they'd hit the comedy clubs after work.

The invitations I liked most of all were to the Friars Club in Manhattan, a kind of frat house for professional comics and others in the entertainment business. For many years, it was a private social club, but later it was opened up to like-minded people in other professions—like ad executives. I was invited to join by Joe LaRosa, and I accepted. That was around the time when the club's roasts started airing on Comedy Central and caught on in popularity. Comics like to tease each other, and people saw how much fun it could be to be teased by experts. Suddenly a line formed to be roasted; would-be victims happily signed up for the privilege. For someone who needs to be the center of attention, a roast is like water to a man lost in the desert.

I didn't particularly need to be roasted, but I enjoyed sitting near the center of the action. I learned a great deal, like that the sound of a joke matters as much as the words—more, sometimes. In recent years, I've turned a few social gatherings into informal roasts, always making sure that the "roastee" is in on the joke and welcomes the attention. So far, everyone has to a greater or lesser degree been fine. I also have a cardinal rule that I don't pick on children or disclose secrets.

I learned quite a bit about humor from some of the great ad execs I've worked for, some of whom were and are absolutely hilarious. Jay Chiat was one of the funniest people I ever met. He wasn't a joke teller so much as someone who recognized absurdity when he saw it and turned it to his advantage. He could do something crazy in such a way that you laughed at the insanity too. Jay was a master of using humor to disarm people and make common cause with them—as Jay taught me, you can't stay angry with someone who cracks you up.

Quite often some of the funniest things are said unintentionally. I had a woman who worked for me for many years who kept me, my staff, and plenty of clients roaring with laughter. She was a delightful lady who was extremely loyal and dedicated but susceptible to verbal bloopers:

"Can you cut a check for $65,000?" I asked her once. "It's for my new golf club."

"$65,000 for a club?" she said. "How much does the whole set cost?"

But wait, there's more!

"Can you bring us some ice, please?" I asked on a different occasion.

"No, I'm afraid not," she said.

"Don't we have ice?"

"We have ice, but it isn't hard yet." (In the olden days, we filled trays with water to put into the freezer.)

My favorite was when she left me voice mails asking me to check my voice mails. The first few times she did this, I brought it up with her that it made no sense. She nodded and promised she wouldn't do it again. She'd always forget. Sometimes I think she did it to make me laugh. It worked.

CHAPTER 23

NO JERKS ALLOWED

DAVID'S RULES FOR BUSINESS, MANAGEMENT, AND THE REST OF LIFE

I do not do well with the "takers," people who only take. I do very well, however, with people who practice their profession or craft with a passion and a commitment to do well for their clients. I have been fortunate to have worked with relatively few people of the former group and with many of the latter group. I think it is not naïve to believe that generosity, consideration, respect, and fairness are repaid many times over. Those who succeed in business and in life most often have an abundance of those traits, and while life is not always fair, it typically works out.

EXAMPLES OF THE TAKERS

I have had potential clients take up my time and not even bother to return a phone call or an email, which is incredible considering their business is client service.

I had a client who sold his business for many millions of dollars insist that I give him a discount since he no longer had a business to pay the fees. I resigned and never looked back, but his partners and relatives retained our services for many years.

I had a client who replaced us with another firm on a temporary CFO's recommendation after the prior CFO was proven to have been incompetent and dishonest and after we saved the firm hundreds of thousands of dollars in taxes. He subsequently hired us back. I then told him he was indeed a mensch.

I had an employee who was highly recommended to me try to take a client for his "moonlighting" practice by offering to do the work for less. He was shocked when I summarily fired him after the client informed me.

I had a client who eventually became a friend who did not want to pay the tax on income for stock options he exercised because the stock subsequently went down. He retained someone else, who prepared the tax returns improperly and, incredibly, blamed me when the client was forced to pay the tax and interest and penalties. I slept well that night.

I had a client whose whole tenure was the span of a lunch—he retained me during the salad portion, and I resigned during the main course, when he said one of his proudest moments was when he found all his tires slashed after a round of staff terminations.

I had a client who said he'd get me a round of golf at Augusta if I waived a fee for a project I did for him related to an investment. I agreed, but there was never a round, not even a golf shirt or any sense of shame on his part. (I did feel a bit less aggrieved when his investment in the project went bad.)

I was invited to speak at a law firm's conference in San Francisco on advertising agency M&A. I was told that the firm would provide lunch but the travel and hotel costs were on my dime. I went, but my role was relegated to answering questions from the audience on accounting, sales tax, and the like.

I had a client who insisted that I advocate a position that I felt was wrong. I asked him, "How is that fair?" and he replied, "Why is that relevant?"

I was offered a bribe twice in my career—both times by the same person. The man wanted me to persuade a client to use his software for the agency's systems. I refused and told the client, but the man denied it. Another lunch was set up for the three of us, and when the client went to the men's room, the man upped the offer. I left the table.

I had a client who had no sports marketing experience but told a prospective buyer that while he had no sports marketing experience or clients, he was a sports fan, so he should be an attractive acquisition.

I had a client who told me that I should give him a discount on my fees due to the experience I would get working for him.

I had a client who informed me that his accountant was terrific because he always got him a tax refund.

One client said that his lawyer told him that he could do a better job than an industry-experienced lawyer since he had no prior commitments.

One client said that her husband was the CFO, and when I asked him if the financial statements were prepared under GAAP, he asked me to fax him the GAAP so that he could verify it.

One client said that there was no need to return media credits or rebates to clients, as they did not know about them or they were not material to the clients.

One client thought nothing of firing me because I refused to omit gains on stock options in his tax return because he felt it was unfair, as the stock imploded after he exercised the options.

One client thought nothing of accepting several invitations to Friars Club Roasts, but when I was not going to one, he would not buy his own tickets, as they were too expensive—it was OK so long as I paid.

I saved one client from personal bankruptcy, and he even sent me a thank-you trophy, but he soon thereafter fired me because his former accountant was cheaper.

I had a client who seems to believe he is a legend and an industry icon. His website says so under an old photo of him.

My client and friend Barrie Hedge is almost exactly the same age as me. On reaching fifty, he gave himself the gift of serenity by giving himself permission to refuse to go along with things others demanded but that he loathed. He allowed two exemptions: The first was for tasks that required two hours of time or less. The second was for tasks that paid exceptionally well. I loved the idea and adopted it immediately. Note that the "gift" is now twenty years old and is nonrefundable and nonexchangeable.

I made some minor adjustments to my gift—I will not work on a matter or participate in a transaction if certain people are involved on either side of the table. I called my version the "no jerk" rule, as in no jerks for clients. (In conversation, I use a different word, but you get the idea.) A few jerks have managed to slip by my radar since then, unfortunately. But when they showed their true colors, I showed them the door. As I get older, my jerk detection system continues to improve. It's a compensation for aging that I've come to appreciate.

I apply this philosophy widely across business and managerial settings. I actually have a hard time separating my business philosophy from my management philosophy. Managing my practice and managing my clients are similar. All I can add in deal situations is to "tell the truth in the most favorable light possible," have reasonable expectations financially and operationally, and try to make sure that every transaction is ultimately successful for both buyer and seller.

As I have matured and learned more about both business and life, I have become less economically fearful and defensive. This has made compliance with my no-jerk rule quite a bit easier. Fools, I've come to realize, thrive on our defensiveness, fears, and insecurities. Those qualities are to idiots what peanut butter on turkey is to rats. Know yourself and respect your own needs, and the jerks will not be able to enter your premises. Got it? Good. Now make it happen.

I am approaching my fiftieth year in business. Whew! Thinking back on the lessons I learned when I was wet behind the ears, it strikes me that the technologies, financial methodologies, and expectation levels when I cashed my first paycheck were profoundly different than today. Meanwhile, the underlying interpersonal dynamics—the methods of creating and managing relationships—are fundamentally unchanged.

The goal in business is to bring in more money than you spend over the long run. To do that, you need to obtain the cooperation, support, and goodwill of many people. I'm generally not sentimental; I don't think making money was necessarily easier in the old days or that people were intrinsically nicer, more honest, or more loyal—it's probably easier to turn a buck today than it was in earlier times.

Preparation is easier today. You can learn more about the people you want to do business with by spending an hour on the internet than you could in a week making phone calls or buttonholing people.

Few people become successful entirely on their own. Most successful businesspeople are highly successful managers. The following are some of the core beliefs that have guided me in assembling, motivating, and keeping my team intact:

- Accessibility trumps weakness.
- Be the hardest worker.
- Arrive early and stay late.
- Give spot bonuses and gifts.
- Don't ask anyone to do anything you would not do yourself.
- Don't flaunt your financial success, but be sure your staff is aware of it.
- Hire the smartest people you can and pay them more than what is reasonably expected.
- Value loyalty and fidelity.
- Expect your staff to work at their *career*, not at their *job*.
- Be sure clients treat staff with respect and vice versa.
- Say "please" and "thank you" all the time.
- Responsiveness overcomes many negatives.
- Give opinions honestly, frankly, and immediately.
- Express your thoughts and opinions with clarity and conciseness. If you cannot explain your reasoning, it won't hold water with clients or staff.
- Develop a sense of humor. Make it suitable for yourself based on your personality.
- Communicate, communicate, communicate.
- Acknowledge others' life events with cards, letters, phone calls, emails, donations, flowers, or gifts.
- Ask for referrals and recommendations and thank any who give them to you.
- Be prepared. Know the facts better than anyone else.
- Drop names only if they give you credibility and a reference.
- Read every document. Never assume an unread document is OK.
- Don't depend on the work of others. Know what you need to know yourself.
- Assess every client's or deal partner's upside and downside tolerance for risk.
- Look after the client's needs. Don't lump those needs together with your own.
- Be objective as to the client's welfare. Don't generate unnecessary fees, ever.

- Be efficient. Do what you need to do quickly, simply, and directly.
- Know that in "creativity," past methods are instructive rather than determinative or prescriptive.
- Draw from your experiences to compose the deliverables.
- Many deliverables should be oral, presented in person, or supplemented in writing.
- Speak plain English. Use technical jargon sparingly or as reference points.
- Don't let a client feign ignorance or stupidity forever. Faked stupidity is worse than the real thing.
- Reciprocate the client's respect. Don't exceed it without getting the equivalent in return. Remember the 80/20 rule: 80 percent of the good comes from 20 percent of the client base, 80 percent of the bad comes from a different 20 percent of the client base, and the other 60 percent of the client base is just OK. Recent studies suggest 90/10 might be more accurate.
- Rate your clients on three scales: quality of work, quality of relationship, and quality of prospects.
- Treat people with the level of respect they deserve as people, not the level you perceive their social status or occupational standing entitles them to.
- Mistakes are easier to deal with than cover-ups. Ask Richard M. Nixon.
- Ending a client or other relationship for good reasons is better than continuing it for bad reasons. It's better for both of you.
- Ask questions until you understand or you can make others understand—do not be embarrassed by your lack of experience or understanding.
- Charge what you are worth in the marketplace to good clients—not the bad 20 percent.
- Appreciate your clients. Referrals from successful clients are your top marketing tools.

CHAPTER 24

AROUND THE OFFICE, OVER THE YEARS

A client gave me this clock to commemorate the closing of a deal
I advised her not to do. She inscribed it with "Time Will Tell." I
clearly attract clients who share my arch sense of humor.

Well ahead of my fiftieth birthday, I found myself thinking about where
my business was going. Years before, when Sydney Hyman departed with
his inventory of new stationery, I told myself I was finished with equal
business partnerships. Throughout my forties, I not only enjoyed the
sense of independence I had earned but came to feel it was essential to
my sense of well-being.

Around this time, I was introduced to Tom Marino, a delightful guy
who was CEO of the accounting firm J. H. Cohn. The two of us got along
well, and he brought up the possibility of combining our firms fairly quickly.

(As an aside, Tom arranged for the proceeds of the sales of old computers and peripherals to be donated to the Benjamin Wiener Foundation.)

After so many years helping others sell their businesses, the time had come for me to sell mine. I was facing my fiftieth birthday, our lease was just about to expire, and my partners were anxious that I might go to work elsewhere, likely at an ad agency, without them, so I committed to finding the right opportunity for us all.

While I had not entirely lost my appreciation for professional autonomy, I also recognized the benefits that a merger would bring. Tom and I explored a deal in more detail. We both agreed that a larger platform would allow us to service a broader range of clients, enable J. H. Cohn to gain expertise in a new industry, and enhance their M&A skills. My firm would benefit from access to the administrative and other support services Tom's firm would supply.

In 1997, J. H. Cohn LLP bought my firm, and we were renamed David C. Wiener and Company—a Division of J. H. Cohn LLP. I came in as a partner and brought along with me my three key professionals: Warren Suna, Harold Goldman, and Bruce Baron.

Bruce, a former frat brother of mine who had become an accountant with my encouragement many years earlier, left my group in 2000 and went to work for J. H. Cohn; he left there about 2003. Arlene Reiser, Karen Sellers, and Mary Policastri also made the transition as employees. Arlene and Mary have since retired.

Carey Gertler joined us after Bruce left and became a partner several years later.

J. H. Cohn went through a merger in 2012 and became CohnReznick. My division remained intact, but after eighteen successful years, I felt that it was time to move on. On October 31, 2014, CohnReznick and I parted ways.

In the summer of 2014, I met Howard Cohen, then COO of EisnerAmper LLP, the estimable accounting and consulting services firm based in Manhattan and Iselin, New Jersey. Howie introduced me to Jay Weinstein, the firm's managing partner for its New Jersey office.

My initial impression was positive. I sensed this firm was quick moving and sensitive to the work-life balance needs and the professional requirements of its partners and staff. I felt there would be great synergy—there's that word again—between their culture and operations and ours. Their policies toward division autonomy, mandatory retirement, telecommuting, and pricing were described to me, and I liked what I heard.

Jay Weinstein introduced me to Charles Weinstein, the CEO of EisnerAmper. I liked him in an instant. (The two men, by the way, are not related. Charly pronounces his name *Wine-steen*; Jay pronounces his *Wine-styne*.)

It should be noted that Tom Marino gave me a wonderful reference even though I was leaving his firm. And Steve Felsher also "perjured" himself for my benefit.

On November 1, 2014, David Wiener and Company LLC was established and became an affiliate of EisnerAmper LLP. Harold Goldman, Warren Suna, Carey Gertler, and Karen Sellers came over with me. This provided continuity for ourselves as well as our clients. As with all human activities, of course, change is inevitable. In October 2016, we wished Warren Suna a happy retirement. Warren is extremely detail oriented, a terrific technician, a warm and empathetic human being—and a great accountant.

Harold Goldman has thrived in our new environment and continues to grow professionally and as a human being. I value him as a colleague and friend. Carey has also thrived. He is a great accountant who, relatively speaking, is still the "kid" on our team.

We recently marked the three-year anniversary of our affiliation. After you've been around for seventy years, three years pass with the blink of an eye. Yet I've already developed warm relationships with Charly, Jay, and some of EisnerAmper's other partners and colleagues. They respect what we do, keep their word, and preserve the firm's admirable culture and values. I've enjoyed my interactions with Mike Aversa, who runs Eisner-Amper's Private Business Services unit, which handles family businesses and smaller accounts, and Pete Bible, the risk management partner. Pete is smart, fair, and practical. Linda Palombi, my current assistant, has learned to read the squiggles I call handwriting and has my back when it comes to documents and the like; she helped a great deal with the preparations of this book.

At this stage of my life, I don't need to be under anyone's feet or take up too much space in anyone's office suite. Telephones, the internet, encrypted technology, Skype, and the cloud allow us to work remotely. My commute is a flight of stairs to get to my fully equipped home office, and I'm good with that.

CHAPTER 25

THIS MESSAGE IS BROUGHT TO YOU BY OUR SPONSORS

When someone asks what I do, I say I'm a CPA. When someone asks what industry I generally work in, I reply advertising.

When I say advertising, I don't mean to slight public relations, media buying, digital media, and all the other estimable specialties and niche businesses that share the rubric "marketing services." But advertising exerts a glamour that to me has never worn off, despite having watched professionals "make the sausage," as the saying goes, for decades.

I enjoy the advertising and marketing communications industries for multiple reasons, one of which is the extraordinary diversity of talent I've encountered and continue to meet up with regularly. These talented people overcome differences in age, education, religion, and sexual preferences to work collaboratively and creatively toward a common goal.

Having worked in close quarters with so many brilliant ad people, I've become highly aware of how advertising dominates our lives. Two generations ago, the average person was exposed to hundreds of commercial messages a day in newspapers, on TV, over the radio, in the mail, and so on. A generation later, the average number was one to two thousand. Thanks to the growth of digital media, robocalls, email solicitations, and more, a person today is exposed to upward of ten thousand commercial messages each and every day.

Being hyperaware of advertising as I am, I can't help but notice the quality of these ads. This is not to say that all those thousands of messages that greet me daily are top notch; some of what passes for commercial messaging is dreadful. But much of it is quite good.

About thirty-five years ago, Jay Chiat assured me I'd never become a competent judge of creative work. Jay said I'd learn what I liked, would figure out what was crap, and had better shut up about the rest of it.

I took his advice. It's served me well.

But after all these years, I figure by now I've earned the right to offer a few thoughts and observations. So here is David Wiener on advertising. What makes for successful advertising? Advertising has to be interesting, entertaining, and—in some circumstances—informative. This directive is more important today than ever. As consumers, we are all besieged with advertising and increasingly able to filter commercials from content, so ad teams need to capture our vastly divided attention and then leave behind a dollop of brand awareness and positive feeling about the sponsor.

The amount of work that goes into creating a simple thirty-second TV commercial would astonish the average person. A single commercial requires the collaboration of writers, graphic artists, actors, directors, set designers, rights specialists, makeup specialists, videographers, and many more. All of these people are specialists in their fields who collaborate for the benefit of the end product.

The most celebrated ad I had the privilege of seeing come together was Chiat/Day's famous "1984" commercial. Perhaps the most famous commercial in history, this spot introduced the Apple Macintosh with an unprecedented riff on Orwellian thought control. The spot, which took on such topics as conformity, autocracy, and the nature of freedom, was developed by Steve Hayden, Brent Thomas, Lee Clow, and many others and directed by Ridley Scott. The commercial was broadcast on January 22 of, yes, 1984, during Super Bowl XVIII on CBS.

As has often been noted, this remarkable commercial was made for a remarkable client. Steve Jobs, the legendary cofounder of Apple, had pressed Jay to create a spot that would stop people in their tracks and change the world. Offering this to Jay was like handing a trumpet to Louis Armstrong. Steve loved the spot Jay created. His board, however, was bitterly divided.

Much of the story behind "1984" has been swallowed by mythology, some of it untrue. Many people believe that the Super Bowl broadcast was the sole airing of the commercial. Not so. Jay made a point of committing to the last spot before midnight on December 31, 1983, on KMVT in Twin Falls, Idaho, so he would qualify for the 1983 advertising awards.

It was also broadcast after the Super Bowl in several small markets. It's hard to say definitively why Jay chose the pattern of ad buys he did. I can't imagine that broadcasting those nine small-market spots made any perceptible impact in terms of market awareness for the brand. I'm inclined to attribute Jay's choice to his unique sense of humor. Jay must have known people would puzzle over his actions and contort themselves into intellectual pretzels trying to figure out what he was thinking. I believe he created a kind of Madison Avenue MacGuffin to confound and perplex those humorless souls who would fixate on it. Jay could have taught Andy Warhol lessons in the art of the put-on.

After those nine spots, the commercial was retired. It has since been endlessly referenced, discussed, studied, and analyzed. TV news broadcasters played the spot over and over after the Super Bowl, providing Apple with more free air time than most clients could imagine purchasing.

The Clio Awards put "1984" in their Hall of Fame. *Advertising Age* named it "Commercial of the Decade" and named Chiat/Day "Agency of the Decade." The accolades continued throughout the years that followed. People still talk about it today. But Jay couldn't have cared less; he rarely bothered to show up to accept the myriad honors, trophies, and plaques the industry bestowed on him. Instead, he sent employees who liked that kind of thing. When he did attend the events, he typically sneaked out early without saying a word, as I mentioned earlier in this book.

Was "1984" the greatest commercial ever made? It's hard to analyze that. What do you think?

The following are some other personal favorite commercials, taglines, and campaigns from over the years:

"I Love L.A." billboard campaign for the 1984 Olympics. Client: Nike. Agency: Chiat/Day.

"Got Milk?" campaign. Client: California Milk Processing Board.
  Agency: Goodby, Silverstein & Partners.
"Tightest Ship in the Shipping Business" campaign. Client: United
  Parcel Service. Agency: Ammirati & Puris.
"Subservient Chicken" campaign. Client: Burger King. Agency:
  Crispin Porter + Bogusky.
"Where's the Beef?" campaign. Client: Wendy's. Agency: Dancer
  Fitzgerald Sample. Special nod to Cliff Freeman.
"Let's Motor" campaign. Client: BMW. Agency: Crispin Porter +
  Bogusky.
"Dumbwaiter" campaign. Client: NYNEX. Agency: Chiat/Day.
"I Can See Clearly Now" campaign. Client: Blind Children's Center
  of Los Angeles. Agency: Chiat/Day.
"Earth's First Soft Drink" campaign. Client: Perrier. Agency: Waring
  & LaRosa.
Samsung Galaxy campaign mocking Apple products. Client: Sam-
  sung. Agency: 72andSunny.

Good ads are simple, entertaining, sometimes moving, and always
memorable. The best ads differentiate their products, brands, and services, making them easy to identify and recall.

Helping marketers build customer bases is of course the industry's
bread and butter. But what's often overlooked is that a huge amount of
advertising is intended not to sell products but to change the way people
think about social issues. Ads, whether paid for by activists, nonprofit
organizations, or socially conscious agency heads, are among the great
drivers of social change around the world. Every day, advertisements
send messages to improve societal issues and health care, promote civil
rights and diversity, and provide relief for the victims of natural disasters.
In recent years, the ad industry has created campaigns to address bullying, domestic violence, animal cruelty, forest fires, drug use, the dangers
of smoking, and so many other worthy causes.

Diversity is a cause that many ad executives have taken to heart. A
generation ago, black Americans were rarely seen in commercials. When

they were, they were usually portrayed in stereotypical roles, doing jobs and performing tasks perceived as unskilled and socially marginal. Today, thanks to initially careful monitoring by the Department of Justice and more recently industry executive commitment, that situation has changed. African Americans are now routinely integrated into settings of every kind. A new generation of Americans has grown up watching blacks participating in fully integrated social situations. African Americans are currently routinely represented as mixed-race couples and parents and economically as managers, professionals, and executives in integrated work settings. Young people today are far more color-blind than their parents or grandparents, a change I attribute in large part to Madison Avenue's leadership and commitment.

Some of my favorite advertisements on social causes are the "Only You Can Prevent Forest Fires" campaign, the "This Is Your Brain on Drugs" campaign, and the Truth campaign about the health risks of smoking.

This business is always evolving. It has evolved from newspapers and magazines to radio, outdoor, TV, internet, digital, and social media. It has evolved from mass media to "on-demand" media, from observational advertising to participatory, from experiential to cause marketing. It has invented product placement, content marketing, and branded content. It has evolved from FSIs (the loose flyers inserted into publications) and mailed coupons to digital and electronic distribution.

It's gone from purchased media to earned and owned media, from relationship-based to qualitative- and results-oriented engagements, from 15 percent commission to negotiated commissions to fee-based, performance-based, and procurement-negotiated compensation. The way advertising works and how agencies are paid are changing all the time.

In addition, the business is an early adopter of new technology and best practices, embracing the use of computers, video, email, HR customs, expense accountability, and new methods of compensating employees. Being exposed to all this has allowed me to see, evaluate, and adopt earlier than most. It has instilled in me an enjoyable sense of what is new and refreshing. It has stimulated my career, my business, and my sense of the world.

Those early perceptions have benefited me socially, professionally, and financially. If people think I'm smart, it's because I've been paying attention to what's gone on around me all these years. I'm far from the only one. Advertising has been and remains an incredible environment to nurture smart people and reward them with positions of responsibility.

Not surprisingly, the business is full of intelligent, ambitious, creative, and hardworking people. I've cherished the open-mindedness, inventiveness, acceptance of new ideas, perceptions, and experiences of so many I've met and worked with. The industry continues to provide me with gratifying client service opportunities, financial rewards, and new and different opportunities. Every day I get to work with some of the most stimulating, challenging, and delightful individuals on the planet. I'm as thrilled to call them colleagues and clients today as I was when I walked into Chiat/Day for the first time in 1981.

I missed advertising's decade of creative revolution in the sixties because I was—damn it!—born too late. But most of the younger giants who dominated Madison Avenue during those glory years—the era that the AMC network so delightfully chronicled in the dramatic series *Mad Men*—were still at the top of their games in the early eighties, when I got my foot in the door.

Jay Chiat, by putting me on Chiat/Day's board, gave me the ultimate credential. His confidence in me ensured I would be taken seriously by the men and women at the industry's top echelons. I knew very little about advertising back then, but that didn't seem to matter. I learned an enormous amount by being part of what was going on at Chiat/Day. Somebody said to me around that time that I was in advertising kindergarten. I replied, "Maybe so, but what a marvelous kindergarten to attend!"

My continuous exposure to such latter-day mad men as Jay Chiat, Martin Puris, Lee Clow, Jeff Goodby, Pat Fallon, and Andy Berlin provided me with a sixth-row seat on the aisle, perfect for watching industry giants do what they do so well. I couldn't help but learn.

One experience I'll never forget was when three of my clients were simultaneously pitching Reebok. The clients were Levine Huntley,

Ammirati & Puris, and Chiat/Day. Each team allowed me to witness parts of their preparations, rehearsals, and pitch meetings, which I watched from behind a one-way mirror. The experience was like getting a PhD in advertising in a few weeks.

The people I've met in this industry over the course of nearly half a century have inspired me many times over. In addition to the legendary agency founders I had the privilege of working with, there are so many executives and creative professionals who stand out in terms of creativity, drive, savvy, and sheer intelligence. There's just not enough space to mention them all.

I strive to stay relevant and enthusiastic by working with exciting, dynamic, creative, and diverse people of all ages. I enjoy every opportunity to collaborate with people who are profoundly knowledgeable and up to date in their areas of expertise and absolutely relish the opportunities to work with people who are newer to the field and who exemplify the novice's characteristic energy. These newcomers are people who don't say "We should—" but rather "What if?" and "Why don't we—?"

Advertising is all about ideas, and the ultimate diversity is the diversity of ideas.

My current clients include many people I've had the opportunity to work with for many years who continue to produce exciting work for their clients: Jeff Goodby, Rich Silverstein, Martin Puris, Richard Kirshenbaum, and Trey Laird, among others. I am also blessed to be able to work with newer clients, including John Boiler, Glenn Cole, Matt Jarvis, Harry Bernstein, Karen Zuckerman, and Linus Karlsson. These bright people and their agencies keep me on my toes, solicit and apply my advice, and keep me at or near the cutting edge of marketing services.

Their agencies—72andSunny; Love the 88; Goodby, Silverstein & Partners; Laird + Partners; Swat; HZDG; Ming; Johannes Leonardo; Crispin Porter + Bogusky; and many others—are all leaders of the current marketing services scene, and I think the scene has never been more interesting.

Their clients include blue chips and companies on the full spectrum who want great strategy, marketing solutions, and the right execution—the ultimate definition of great work. Methods of production and delivering the message to the audience and the speed of work have evolved in a revolutionary sense, but it is a continuing part of the business I admire and tangentially work in.

And of course there are always new companies, new agencies, and new practitioners appearing and making their presences felt. There are media planners who now plan buys on social media sites and there are six-second TV spots and spots that interact with viewers in more experiential ways than before.

Whatever they're doing, it will be different next year and the year after, that's guaranteed.

Many of the professionals I've known continue to do amazing work. One of them is Adelaide Horton. I met Adelaide at Chiat/Day. She moved on to the Lowe Group before returning to Chiat/Day. Eventually she went out on her own as an industry consultant and continues to do very well. This woman is what I call scary smart. She is a delight to work with, is a valuable mentor, and most importantly has become one of my dearest friends. My personal admiration increased when I learned that she had been on the "Miracle on the Hudson" plane when it went down. During that crisis, she again proved her toughness and resilience. Adelaide and her husband, John, have consistently made generous donations to the Benjamin Wiener Foundation as well.

I have worked with and represented some of the first account planners who went on to change the industry. While Jay Chiat was the visionary who brought the discipline to the US from London, these professionals have proved their merit many times over. Included on my A-list are Jane Newman (Chiat/Day, then Merkley Newman Harty), Mary Hermann (who became Mary Puris), Jon Steele, Robin Danielson, and M. T. Rainey.

Throughout the years, I've come to see that the skill set of every successful adman and adwoman includes industrial-strength people skills. I don't just mean the ability to get along with others—to play together nicely in the sandbox, so to speak—although that's handy. I mean the ability to ferret out brilliance, to win over migratory talent, to motivate, to inspire, to coach, to teach, and above all, to lead. The great agency owners are all charismatic leaders who naturally attract and motivate others. When you take the lead and inspire your employees, you attract great clients. Your ads go on to win awards. The recognition attracts great employees; great employees attract more great clients. It's what I call the Virtuous Circle, which I discussed earlier.

I continue to meet great people all the time. Today's young generation of ad execs strikes me as formidable. Many millennials actually have a healthier perception of work-life balance than the boomer execs whose shoes they are now filling. I wish the millennial generation all the best and look forward to being part of the successes I'm sure they will achieve.

CHAPTER 26

MY FAMILY

This award, which was given to me and my wife, Sheila, is especially meaningful to us because it recognizes the importance of Israel and Judaism in our upbringing and family values.

Sheila and I have raised three fantastic kids. They sometimes drive me nuts, but they also make me kvell—Yiddish for "burst with pride."

My three kids always visit Sheila and me and each other on holidays and birthdays.

They are available and supportive when someone in the family needs help (although they may grumble at first).

They accept their positions in life and don't pretend to be what they are not.

They keep in touch consistently—at least with their mother if not with me.

They are honest, have stayed away from drugs and alcohol problems, and are extremely ethical.

Paul's the oldest, named after my mother's uncle, who had a heart condition and severe diabetes, and I knew he wouldn't be around forever. He didn't live to attend my wedding, but before he died, I told him I'd name my first son after him. I think that meant a lot to him.

Paul is extremely independent and self-reliant, though at times, he is disinclined to compromise. Paul grew up with a proclivity for gadgets, electronics, and figuring out how things work. He lives in Astoria, Queens, and works in IT in Manhattan.

Rachel is our second. Rachel knows a great deal about beauty and cosmetics through observation, learning, and experimentation. She has been able to turn her passion into a career, working as an executive in the beauty industry. Rachel is charming, outgoing, funny, incredibly loud, very generous, and fiercely loyal. She lives in Long Island City, New York.

Laura, our third, is a loving and dedicated mother and is smart, intuitive, supportive of her children, and intensely loyal. She navigates incredibly well within the community, dealing adroitly with people who are quite difficult, eccentric, and sometimes quite demanding. She and her loving husband, Robert, have produced three delightful kids: Alexis, Samantha, and Max. And we are blessed in that they live one and a half miles away.

Alexis (Lexi), fourteen, is a dancer. She is petite and very astute. She can read me like a book and, everyone will tell you, has me wrapped around her finger. When she was born, I called her Little Dolly. I still do. Her brain is outsized.

Samantha (Sammi) is a twelve-year-old soccer and lacrosse star and is scary smart. She says things at twelve you wouldn't expect a twenty-five-year-old to say. She is affectionate and happy to show it.

When we had our housewarming party, we gave all the guests T-shirts that my wife designed. The front shows a rendering of our house; the back is self-explanatory. Here are my three grandchildren (Alexis, Samantha, and Max, from left to right). The house is twenty-four years old, older than them, but they know it as Papa and MeeMee's house.

Max is nine, the youngest and the possessor of a great sense of humor. He is also a talented drummer and budding entertainer. At family gatherings, he gets up, sings, dances, and tells jokes. To call him outgoing is to say New York is a big city. He is a bit of an old soul, likely reincarnated from Borscht Belt talent. "Papa," he called out when he overheard me saying something he disagreed with, "what the hell are you drinking?"

Sheila has been my love and the light of my life for more than half a century, putting up graciously with my foibles and ways of doing things that are not always commensurate with hers. We will celebrate our fiftieth wedding anniversary in 2018. She has not worked commercially since 1971, when she took maternity leave. It's been a long leave.

Sheila has been a superb household manager, allowing me to concentrate on business. This division of labor has helped both of us appreciate each other's strengths without becoming entangled in an office setting. Sheila continues to be consistently supportive and an invaluable sounding board. People who meet us often end up describing her as my better half. They're right.

As a coparent, she's been a necessary complement to my philosophy of benign neglect. I was the one to ship the kids off to summer camp every year, to relish the rare moments of calm and quiet. Sheila was the one to assemble care packages that she'd mail to them almost daily. Between the two extremes, I think we raised three great kids.

We were each other's first loves and had a memorable wedding that made our families happy. All my aunts, uncles, and cousins from Brighton

Beach were there. My college friends, Barry Scher, Elliot Zelevanksy, Mel Belitsky, and Bruce Baron, were there. We all stayed in touch for many years, and as mentioned, Bruce eventually came to work for me as an accountant.

However, the honeymoon started on an off-key note. Our travel agent booked us into a hotel near Newark Airport for our wedding night—the problem was that the hotel didn't exist. We found alternate arrangements on our own, but my bride and I deserved better than that. You better believe I gave the travel agent a piece of my mind when I finally got him on the phone. After that there were no major problems. All the subsequent hotels turned out to actually exist and accommodated us as per plan.

We went to California and Las Vegas, did the usual tourist things, and acted like typical honeymooners, except for my making a few detours to see clients. If nothing else, my behavior alerted Sheila to what kind of a man she'd married. She took it in stride.

As for the marriage, it's been a marvelous ride. I'd say marrying Sheila was the best choice I've made. As to why she married me, you'd have to ask her.

Like many Americans, I'm inclined to spend too many hours at work and not enough time with my family. I've consciously tried to balance work and life, with moderate success. For quite a few years, I've spent more time working remotely, coming into the firm's office only when absolutely necessary. I'm every bit as accessible through phones, Skype, and email as I am when I'm in the office proper. I get more work done too, as there are fewer distractions. I still put in the hours, but somehow it's easier to take when you're at home and your commute is a minute or less.

What does the future hold? A friend of mine, a retired surgeon, called the other day and told me he's lost the ability to sit and do nothing, something he had enjoyed at the onset of his recent retirement. He asked me how I was doing. I told him that I've never had the ability to sit and do nothing and didn't think I'd develop it. At some point I'm going to retire, but that's not in the cards right now. I'm too busy enjoying myself to retire. But I am quite sure I would fail at retirement. In fact, when I joined EisnerAmper LLP in 2014, I committed to them for thirty years, at which point I will be ninety-seven.

At that time, I said to them, we'll have to take it a year at a time.

On the wall above my desk sits a set of encyclopedias. This set is admittedly from the days when every middle- and working-class Jewish family managed to set aside enough money for a down payment to buy them on an installment plan.

Not long ago, Lexi strolled into my office, providing a happy momentary distraction. "Papa," she asked, pointing at the encyclopedias, "what are those?"

To her generation, knowledge is contained on electronic devices, not within a set of hardcover books.

When I showed her what encyclopedias are, she asked if I read all the books. I told her I had, and she asked why I still keep my old set. I wanted to explain that when I was her age, my aunt's set of encyclopedias opened my eyes to a world far beyond Brighton Beach. A passion for knowledge, the God-given brains to use it, and the highest expectations for myself and those around me have been the foundation on which my life has been based. What success I've enjoyed, what benefits I've brought to others, what joy I've found and shared in this journey have been based primarily on this foundation.

I didn't say any of this, of course. I just smiled and said, "Oh, they hold memories."

I look forward to seeing this book take its place on my shelf and hopefully the shelves of my children and grandchildren. It should put to rest the question of why Papa/Dad still keeps a set of encyclopedias in his office, and perhaps a few other questions too.

I hope it will serve to gently open their eyes to the world I know. I'm seventy years old, and much of the world of my youth is gone now in the physical sense. Yet that world lives on vibrantly in my head and my heart in the form of the lessons, advice, warnings, laughter, tears, generosity of spirit, and words of inspiration from so many people I've had the privilege of knowing and loving, sometimes antagonizing, sometimes delighting, who taught me much more than they realize.

CHAPTER 27

YEAH? SAYS WHO?

I have been blessed with good health, and I have directed many of my charitable efforts toward trying to ensure good health for others. This award recognizes my funding of a patient assistance program for people battling lymphoma, as my mother did before her passing.

My life's journey has followed the path from Brighton Beach Avenue in Brooklyn to Madison Avenue in Manhattan. As the crow flies, this is a journey of little more than twenty miles, but I've made so many stops along the way—and I'm still making them. My journey has taken me across New York City and around the world. I've gone to Moscow and negotiated trade deals in the Kremlin. I've been to Los Angeles, San Francisco, and Venice, California, many times, where I helped the brilliant Jay Chiat bring an "outsider's view" of business and financial discipline to the agency.

I've been to Miami, Toronto, Minneapolis, Detroit, Sydney, Zurich, London, Rome, and many places in between. I've gone very often to Hawaii, where I play golf near a dormant volcano. Through all the travel, my home base remained in New Jersey—initially Somerset, then Marlboro, and now Rumson. For about fifty years, here is where I've lived, where I've worked from my home office, and where I've always returned to after traveling to Manhattan.

My beginnings were on Brighton Beach Avenue at Twelfth Street seventy years ago. It was a place where the arc of everyone's life was defined by their origins. You were known by who your parents were, where you lived, who your relatives were, where you went to school, and where your family originally came from. This was both protective and limiting—and I never accepted being limited.

I originally left Brighton Beach to go to Brooklyn College but returned every night. When I graduated, I joined the first wave of baby boomers leaving college, worried about staying out of the escalating Vietnam War, and went out in search of a job.

I had no pedigree, no credentials, no fancy doors to knock on where I could mention my father's name and someone in an expensive suit would smile and ask how Dad was doing or give me a nickname like Skip or Chip or Mack. Nobody gave a crap.

What I did have going for me was that I was a pretty smart Jewish kid with a damp-ink Brooklyn College diploma and some experience working at a small accounting firm on Court Street. After we moved into our offices to Fifth Avenue, when I walked out of the subway near St. Patrick's Cathedral, I might as well have been crossing the Yellow Brick Road. All of a sudden, everything was in Technicolor. The handful of clients we had at the start and the prospects that visited were clearly astounded by our luxurious digs. We may have been *pishers*, but we presented like *machers*. What a difference that made for a pair of newcomers.

Fifth Avenue is one block from Madison Avenue. This location was as close as I've come to having a literal Madison Avenue address. Although today the advertising industry is far more decentralized, the name still conjures up for me the era when Madison Avenue was the red-hot center of the advertising industry and one of the most exciting places to work in America. In my mind, Madison Avenue remains the glamorous corridor where brilliant creatives and clever strategists toil late into the night, creating ads that change how America lives.

I learned so much in those early years on Fifth Avenue from the attorney I shared offices with. I learned to scrutinize every contract, challenge every clause inhospitable to my clients, and just say no to people when they say, "Things are always done this way"; "Just sign. You don't have to read every line"; or, my personal favorite, "You can't change that in the contract! It's always that way."

Yeah? Says who?

The Ostrowitz brothers, who owned Gilbert Plastics, were a pair of tough, unsentimental businessmen who spent not a nickel more than they had to. They did, however, do something wonderful for me. They had confidence in me and demonstrated that confidence by sending me to negotiate their major contracts. The greatest thing you can do for a young person is to give him or her the chance to show what he or she can do. When I set my shingle out on Fifth Avenue, they followed me, becoming my anchor client. Their faith in me bolstered my confidence enormously.

Another person who proved his confidence in me with his actions was Jay Chiat. With Jay business was never just business. It was always somewhat personal. I knew less than nothing about the advertising industry when I met Jay. Didn't matter. Right away, he handed me a series of projects to handle. When I succeeded, he piled on more responsibilities. He always let me do my thing. I was astonished when I learned I was the only outsider Jay named to the board of Chiat/Day.

Most immediately, the move made my work much easier in the company. It's one thing to push back against a part-time accountant, but it is quite another to tangle with a board member with Jay's ear and the equity Jay had bestowed on me. The position also credentialed me to Madison Avenue. On top of that, Jay made many phone calls on my behalf and mailed quite a few personal letters. He opened many doors for me, for which I will be forever grateful.

Our relationship went far beyond business. Jay was the older brother I never had, supportive yet always testing and teasing, refusing to let me or anyone else get complacent. He was the sibling I didn't know I needed: generous, caring, unpredictable, unmanageable, adventurous, narcissistic, hilarious, and irrepressible. He was the most self-contradictory person I've ever known. He was a genius. I'll never forget him.

My beloved parents, Pearl and Benjamin Wiener, had very different attitudes about business and success than I've come to develop, reflecting their own generational backgrounds and unique set of personal experiences. Although my beliefs evolved on the road to Madison Avenue, their influence on me is profound and enduring. They taught me about being faithful and ethical, working hard, and keeping family foremost in mind no matter what. My sweet Zaydeh, my grandfather Nathan, who moved into my bedroom in our little apartment when his wife died, also set the bar high. An émigré from Romania, my grandfather was forced to make many adjustments in the course of his life in order to survive, including, when he was in his seventies, becoming roommates with a yeshiva boy, and he never complained. My aunts and uncles; some of my teachers in yeshiva, Abraham Lincoln High, and Brooklyn College; and the rabbis who passed along the wisdom of our Jewish faith also helped guide, direct, and correct me when necessary, although the latter has never been easy. May they all rest in peace.

I couldn't possibly list all the teachers, mentors, and inspirations in my life; I have learned something from nearly everyone I have ever worked for, supervised, been supervised by, done business with, cussed out, or been cussed out by. I've even learned from my first real employers, who instilled in me the need to be self-sufficient, to force change, and to be self-directing and hardworking. May they rest in peace.

In the process of writing this book, I looked back at my life and career. I'm extremely proud of my accomplishments in business and in family, particularly my marriage of half a century and counting. I am thankful for Sheila's patience, intuition, instincts, faith, and, of course, unconditional love. My wonderful adult children—Paul, Rachel, and Laura—my son-in-law, Robbie; and my precious grandchildren, Lexi, Sammi, and Max, never fail to delight, distract, and instruct.

I've organized my career on the principle that accountants should not limit themselves to pencil pushing and number crunching but contribute strategically to advance the success and achievements of their clients. I believe I've held true to my principle.

I've been fortunate to have been able to provide financial advice and tax and planning services that have helped many people achieve and preserve wealth. I've also been fortunate in being able to help many business-people and entrepreneurs successfully sell their agencies for maximum returns and transition to the next phases of their lives.

I'm blessed to have been able to raise my family in comfortable and secure circumstances, to contribute to the community where I live, and to keep my parents' memory alive through the good works of the Benjamin Wiener Foundation, which helps people with cancer get health care, personal-need services, prescriptions, and other things they require in their time of need.

Back in Brighton Beach, my parents used to keep a set of dishes in the back of a closet, far nicer than the "good china" we reserved for holidays and company. Not long ago, spurred by I don't know what, I found the dishes in our attic, where they hadn't been opened for decades.

I recognized them instantly. They were the "president's china." My mother reserved this service for the most special of special occasions. "We'll keep it nice and use it when the president comes to visit," I remember her saying so many years ago, always with a gentle smile. It was sort of a joke, sort of not. America was then the kind of country where hardworking everyday people could dream of the president dropping in on them. And when that happened, of course they'd have the proper china to serve him dinner.

Sometimes we have to serve ourselves on the president's china. As my parents and so many others inspired me, I look forward to being able to inspire and teach others as I continue to be inspired by and learn from others for, I hope, a long time to come.

MY FAVORITES

Movie: *Animal House*
TV show: *Blue Bloods*
Sports team: New York Giants
Sport I can still attempt to play: Golf
Comedians: Buddy Hackett, George Carlin
Songs: Sinatra's "My Way" and "The Way You Look Tonight"
Dinner: Sushi
Wine: California Cabernet
Cigar: Cohiba
Cliché: "The swimming pool on the Titanic is still full."
Music: The Great American Songbook
Vacation spot: Four Seasons Hualalai in Kona, Hawaii
Heroes:* Jay Chiat, Harry Truman, Jonas Salk, Michael Bloomberg,
    Bill Russell, my grandkids
Clothier: L.L. Bean
Entertainers: Frank Sinatra, Sammy Davis Jr.
Best friend: Sheila, my wife

---

* Each and all of them tell/told the truth, are/were honest, care/cared about superior performance, and have/had no hidden personal agendas. They all care/cared about humanity, the arts, people on a broad scale, their team, and the world.

DAVID WIENER'S NEGOTIATION RULES

Ask the question, Why are we doing this (strategy, cash-out, merger, etc.)?

Agree on a press release in advance as a script that will later be edited. If an agreement is absent at inception, move on. The contents of a press release cover the most important issues—branding, reporting, reasoning, future role of seller, and so on.

Be tough but fair.

Be more prepared than anyone else—know the issues, the importance and relevance of the issues, the accounting, the taxes, the psychology, the numbers, the market values, and so on.

Be honest—no lies, no material omissions, no misleading statements, and no unfair positions.

Agree on one channel of communication.

Be objective—don't fall in love with an idea or a number.

Be prepared to say no, to say yes, to compromise, or to adjourn.

Know the opposing party—their history, experience, style, and preferences—and the scope of the authority of the negotiator.

Keep a sense of humor—this is not life or death.

Keep the client's values and wishes in mind.

Remind the opposing party what is to be accomplished and why the common nonmonetary goal is relevant.

Control the language, monitor and control the lawyers, and modulate the tone of the conversation.

Keep a running list of open items.

Try not to relitigate agreed-upon points, and always have a response if it is attempted by the opposing party (raise new points, raise the price, refuse to go backward).

Make no threats you cannot or will not deliver on.

Be punctual, have a list, make notes, and think through interconnected points.

Win—winning is a necessity.

If the opposing person is making a big mistake, ask if he or she is prepared to commit to it and give him or her an option to rethink it. If realized later on, the negotiation will become difficult, and the deal is more likely to die.

Set expectations for your client beforehand (terms, pricing, postclosing role, press reaction).

Think about communication to all stakeholders (buyer, seller, clients, employees, industry, family, etc.).

QUESTIONS YOU SHOULD ASK YOUR POTENTIAL M&A ADVISOR

Does he or she know the particular issues and styles of each of the strategic buyers, the protections you'd need in a likely earnout or less than 100 percent sale, how and on what to apply to negotiated multiple, how to maximize your earnout potential, and so on?

Does he or she know what was done or not done in other deals?

Does he or she know the pros and cons of the potential buyer, what the potential buyer's reputation is, and what to be careful of?

Does he or she know how to present to a buyer a strategy based on his or her company's holdings and operations?

Does he or she know how to enhance the likelihood of growth from a strategic buyer?

Does he or she know the terms on which capital will be provided postclosing?

Does he or she know each buyer's market level compensation and incentive plans?

Does he or she know the impact of baskets in an earnout?

Does he or she know how to minimize the working capital you will leave behind at closing?

Does he or she know what assets should be retained and what liabilities should be excluded?

Does he or she know what might be done to mitigate SALT (state and local taxes)?

Does he or she know how to treat accounts receivable (especially intercompany), life insurance, audit and tax prep fees, intercompany cost allocations, and so on?

Does he or she believe that at least X percent of value can be added (the amount of his or her fees) over the course of a deal? Recall that if you do an earnout, much of your proceeds will be based on the future. Those payments will be a multiple—likely on a variable grid—on future profits. Many M&A advisers will write a book and send it out to hundreds of possible buyers. They will conduct a broad auction and push for an all-cash 100 percent purchase, which does not always give you the economic benefit of large growth and the probable benefits of a strategic buyer. That process may also deter some buyers. I prefer a narrower, targeted approach and, when it makes sense, a partial sale and/or an earnout.

EXPERIENCES IN BUSINESS

SEYMOUR GRAHAM

Seymour Graham, a tough businessman from Pennsylvania, was one of my early plastics company clients. He would call my office or home and say, "Wiener? Graham"—even though I always knew who it was. One time I asked him why he never asked how I was or talked about anything else. He said, "At your rates per minute, I am not that interested."

But when I was pitching Duane Reade—also tough and price-conscious people—and I used him as a reference, he told them that I represented him for fifteen years, which meant he had received 180 bills from me. Each month, he said, he opened the bill and gasped. But, he added, he would never use anyone else.

Seymour also gave me a free lesson in transparency and how to think about costs. After he completed a large transaction, I sent him a bill for $500,000 and about $2,300 in out-of-pocket costs. He called and asked for the documents to support the out-of-pockets. I asked why and offered to waive them, and he replied, "David, I cannot really assess the value of your services, but I can readily see if you were being honest with me on the out-of-pockets." We sent him the supporting documents, and he wired the $502,300 the next day.

BERNIE MADOFF

I dealt with Bernie Madoff three times over the years.

The first time was when Jay Chiat asked me to come to a meeting at Chiat/Day. He met a guy at his golf club in the Hamptons who was being lauded by many as a money wizard. I went to the meeting, and

Madoff and a colleague of his were there to meet with Jay and me. I had never heard of Madoff before then but had researched him a bit.

When Jay introduced me, Madoff told me to call him Bernie. Jay told me he was thinking of investing some money with Madoff, but he did not understand what Madoff's investment program was.

Madoff proceeded to double-talk and speak in confusing lingo. Jay asked if I understood it, and I said no, so Jay got up and said that he was going to get coffee and that when he came back, we'd try again.

As he was leaving the room, Jay also threw out that his own mother convinced him that he was in the 51 percentile of intelligence. And he told Madoff that I was in the 52 percentile, which meant more than half the world was dumber than us.

Jay came back, and I asked Madoff, "Suppose we give you $100,000 to invest. What will you do with the money?" He said he'd buy options and hedge the funds so that money was to be made regardless of the market's direction. I asked follow-up questions, but the response was pure babble.

Jay passed on the investment opportunity.

My second interaction was when Madoff—who loved taking money from Jewish and Israeli charities—proposed to the Weizmann Institute that if he was given $50 million to invest, he'd assure us of $5 million in donations.

In hindsight, a Ponzi scheme of ten to one is quite good.

The investment committee consisted of some very smart people, including myself, and we did not understand what he did and how he accomplished his claimed results, and so we passed.

My third interaction involved Bob Ingram, who had invested much of his portfolio with Madoff on the advice of some of Bob's wealthy friends.

Note that most of their wealth was lost.

We received a K-1 form for Bob's income taxes, and it made no sense. We called Madoff's office and were told to call the outside CPA firm, who could not explain it and asked us what we thought it should be. The firm was the subject of a great deal of press.

We recommended that Bob get out his money, which he did. However, the timing was too close to the collapse, and he was forced to settle with the trustee and return part of the money.

Subsequent events, litigation, and disclosures proved the obvious—if you listened and thought about his sales pitch on an objective basis, a reasonable person would not have invested.

He was a fraud and a thief, but he was a smart marketer and appealed to greed and insecurity and used the scarcity of opportunity and informal social marketing to get more victims. He utilized word-of-mouth advertising to help him raise billions of dollars.

Fool's gold!

BRUCE SPRINGSTEEN

Many people identify the "Boss" with New Jersey and, specifically, the town of Rumson, where I live. I never cared for his musical style.

On a flight to Newark from Los Angeles one day, as I sat in my aisle seat, I turned to the person sitting next to me, who was in jeans and a T-shirt, and nodded at him. Then I started to read my book. Throughout the flight, I noticed the flight attendants, passengers, and flight crew kept walking by my seat and staring. I checked my fly, my nose, and my hair, and all seemed fine.

I asked my seatmate what was going on, and he explained that he was Bruce Springsteen. When I told him what I do, he said M&A guys make tons of money. I told him I had a pretty good year, but I heard he had a pretty good weekend.

MILES NADAL

Miles Nadal had asked me for any suggestions of media-buying companies he might be able to acquire to build scale. One of the companies I suggested was RJ Palmer.

MDC, Miles's company, did, in fact, acquire it, and I did not know about it until it was in the press. I called Miles and told him I was annoyed because I did not represent MDC, nor did I have an opportunity to represent the seller. Miles laughed and said he was going to send me $50,000—he said it was pure profit to me and that he saved much more by my not representing the seller.

Miles called me one day and asked if I was able to go on a golf trip to Pebble Beach with him and some other MDC people. He said that MDC would cover the cost and that all I had to do was get myself out there.

When I arrived, I found out that Miles could not make it and that I was taking his place. Miles is a mensch. I had a good time socializing with MDC employees, whom I only ever saw in the office.

At one event with my family, Miles called several times and interrupted the festivities. He apologized after and sent us a batch of iPads as gifts—back when they were not as widely used as they are now.

Miles also was of the opinion that one should not pay someone merely for an introduction. I agree!

Miles has an incredible eye for talent and potential, as evidenced by his acquisitions of 72andSunny, Crispin Porter + Bogusky, Anomaly, Mono, and so on. He is not perfect, but not every NFL first-round draft choice becomes a star.

MADELINE DEVRIES

Madeline DeVries was recommended to me by George Fertitta and Marina Maher. She owned a PR firm that specialized in women's products. P&G was a big client of hers, and she was and is quite elegant and proper.

It was an interesting dynamic between us. After the sale to IPG, we celebrated with our spouses at the Friars Club. Madeline had never been there and was fascinated by the environment and the reputation of the club.

At dinner, the dean of the club, Freddie Roman, came over, and we chatted. Madeline mentioned she was a fan of Milton Berle ever since she was a child.

It is a legend in the entertainment business that Uncle Miltie had a huge penis—the club called it Big Miltie.

Freddie proceeded to tell us the story of Milton and Charlie Callas, who also claimed to be well endowed. One night, the bragging was too much, and the two contenders decided to have a face-off upstairs in the gym. They both came out in their robes, and Callas exposed himself to gasps.

Milton looked, smiled, and said, "Not bad. All I'll do is take out enough to beat you."

Madeline smiled, blushed, and looked away while Sheila, Ian—her husband—and I cracked up.

DALE ADAMS

I was in the last stages of selling an agency to Omnicom. My client had taken as part of his past fees several photographs from famous people, which belonged to the seller. The collection was on the walls of his office and was worth many hundreds of thousands of dollars.

We listed the art as "excluded assets"—my client would keep ownership, and they would not be part of the deal.

The point person for the buyer objected. I asked, "If we had owned a Rembrandt, would you expect to get it?" He insisted that the photographs were part of the office's decor.

I called Dale Adams, his superior, and Dale set up a conference call. Dale asked the point person how much he budgeted for decorative art and how many items there were.

I think there were sixteen items, and the budget was $150 per decorative piece. Dale asked me to concede $2,400, or sixteen times $150. I did, and we further agreed that the art would be left in place for so long as my client was employed and that Omnicom would pay $1 per year plus the cost of insuring the pieces.

Twenty minutes and done.

Dale is a really smart and fair guy.

FRED MEYER

The late Fred Meyer was the CFO of Omnicom. He was a wonderful and brilliant man who taught me a great deal about M&A, the advertising business, and life. I admired him and think of him quite often.

One time, after we had agreed on a sale transaction, a problem arose. My client had been charging many of the selling agency's purchases on his personal credit card so he could get the miles. I told him that would have to stop after the sale, and he was very upset; the miles were what he used to pay for his family's Christmas holiday trip.

Fred asked me how the deal was progressing, and I told him we were three million miles apart. Fred smiled and increased the salary of the seller's principal to compensate him for the miles' value.

In another transaction, Omnicom was under severe time pressure to have a solution in place to solve a client conflict. I met with my client and walked to Omnicom's offices. Fred and I agreed on a terms sheet in forty-five minutes, including coffee and small chat.

I couldn't go back to my new client's offices so quickly—typically a deal takes weeks, so a new client may think I agreed too easily—so I stopped and bought a pair of golf shoes, had a hamburger, and then strolled back to my client's offices. The client was shocked that the deal was made in less than two hours. It was, indeed.

JAY CHIAT

When I arrived at Chiat/Day one morning, Jay Chiat asked me to walk a few blocks north to meet with an agency that had its largest client file for bankruptcy the prior evening. Jay said the agency was "in trouble" and that he'd be willing to invest about $1 million if it would help them survive but did not want to waste the money if it was hopeless.

I walked over to the agency and met with the principals and the CFO. To say they were unrealistic and unwilling to accept reality or to make painful changes is a gross understatement, and I told them so. As I walked back into Jay's office, he had them on speakerphone.

They told Jay that I was rude, opinionated, crude, loud, and stupid.

Jay responded with "He's not stupid."

So much for my great friend defending me.

Note that the agency closed down within a few months.

CHUCK PORTER

Some years after the sale to MDC, Crispin Porter enjoyed great success. I felt I contributed in some small way to that, and I asked Chuck to consider a special fee in recognition.

A few days later, a check arrived for the $150,000 I suggested.

BOB INGRAM

Bob Ingram was a great client, a fellow Friars Club member, and a source of unending stories. He was always into the latest technology and gadgets. After I completed a project for him with very good results, he sent me a large Sony flat-screen TV that was not yet available to the public.

I had to hire an installation company from Queens to remove my old TV, install the new one, and bring all the required accessories (speakers, amps, etc.). Then Sheila decided it was a good idea for the old TV to be installed in my daughter's apartment in New York. Long story short, the free TV cost me more than Bob paid for it, but at least Rachel and I had new TVs.

Note that my TV watching consists of NFL games and five to six hours per year of other shows. I am not a movie watcher, a video game player, or a TV show addict. Part of the reason is that TV, for me, is as good as an instant-acting sleeping pill.

MR. AND MRS. SMITH

Sheila and I were invited to John and Jane's wedding. He was married before; she was not. She was/is much younger than John and was quite wealthy.

The Friday before the wedding, John asked me to come to a meeting at his office with him and Jane. When I went, she was distressed and was wearing huge sunglasses to hide red eyes. They could not agree on a prenup, and the two sides' lawyers were unable to come to terms. I was asked to suggest terms, since they both trusted me, and I did. The wedding took place per schedule.

Some twenty years later, they are still married and have children, and all seems well.

Note a somewhat similar situation arose with another client where the circumstances were similar but where the husband had older children from a prior marriage. Same result—they are still married and have children, and no one looks at the prenup, which I suggested dissolve after X years of marriage and/or a child was born.

MARTY GOLDMAN

Marty Goldman was a client and was the CEO of a plastic hanger manufacturer. Marty had a factory in New Rochelle, New York, and one in Pennsylvania. He had spent some time in prison years before I knew him for a nonviolent crime. He also had ulcers and ate a lot of cereal and milk.

One day in his office, he was pouring himself a bowl of cereal, and a mouse fell out of the box and ran away. He ate the cereal anyway without giving it another thought—he was even shocked when I declined a bowl.

Some years later, I had to sue Marty for unpaid fees. We won a judgment, and when I tried to enforce it, his lawyer informed us that Marty was diagnosed with liver cancer. My lawyer asked if I would lay off, and I said it was likely a lie and to ask for a physician's letter to prove it. No letter ever came—he was cured!

LET'S CALL HIM SAM

One of Marty Goldman's colleagues was the plant manager of both of Marty's factories—we'll call him Sam. One day, Sam had a gallbladder attack and was taken for surgery to a New York hospital. I went to visit him and met his wife, who was in his room.

He asked me to go to the cafeteria and get him something to eat, and when I returned to his room, his "wife" was there, but it was a different woman. This different woman also had the same first name as the woman I met earlier.

When I was alone with him, he told me he had two families, two sets of kids, and two homes, one in Pennsylvania and one in Long Island.

He had no shame, no fear, and no concern.

I asked how he kept it a secret. He said few knew of it; neither wife had any income, so there were no income tax issues; and the second wife had separate health insurance for her and the children. Finally, he said that when he died, it wouldn't be his problem anymore.

SYDNEY HYMAN

Sydney Hyman was one of the brightest people I ever knew. But one day, he had to go to court in New Jersey and asked to borrow my car. He took it out of the garage near our Fifth Avenue office, drove it to Newark, and parked it in a garage. When he returned to the office, he told me that he went to the Newark garage, the attendant pointed to the car, and Sydney got in and drove off.

He soon realized it was the wrong car.

When he drove back to the garage and told the attendant he made an error, the attendant said, "Just put it back. No one will know." True, except Sydney filled the wrong car's gas tank.

YEHOCHAI "JOE" SCHNEIDER

Yehochai "Joe" Schneider was a client for many years and in many ventures. I met him through Milton Ostrowitz of Gilbert Plastics. Joe is an engineer, a consummate entrepreneur, an Israeli, and quite eccentric. He kept his office at sixty-five degrees to keep people awake. He rolled his own cigars from leaf and ground tobacco. He had little shame and did not like to waste money.

He and I once took a redeye flight from LAX to JFK. We were expected to land at about six o'clock in the morning, and we had a meeting later that morning in New York City. On the plane, he asked me if I wanted the upper or the lower. I didn't know what he meant, so I said the upper. Then he got down on the floor with a pillow and two blankets, got himself into the shape of a *C*, and went to sleep, head under one seat, legs under the other. We were in first class but . . .

When we landed, he asked what I was going to do for the next few hours. I told him that I was going to get a hotel room, shower, nap, and change my clothes.

He said that I was being wasteful, then he went into the airline club's men's room, got naked, sat on the counter with his feet in one sink and his ass in another, and bathed. Then he shaved and dressed—no shame, no concern. I was astounded, but the looks on the faces of the other men in the men's room were priceless.

After his involvement with some people I did not feel comfortable with, we went our separate ways, but he had always treated me fairly—and clearly, kept things interesting.

A SMALL CONNECTICUT AGENCY

A client asked me to meet a friend of his who owned a small agency in Connecticut. I agreed to go as a favor, and when I contacted this person, we decided to meet at his office in Connecticut at about 6:30 p.m. As I was leaving Manhattan, it began to snow. Note that a flight home from London is quicker than a drive to New Jersey from Connecticut in the snow.

As I arrived at his office, the snow was piling up. We began the meeting, and after twenty minutes or so, as I was describing some aspects of my credentials and experience, I realized he had dozed off. I called his name and shook him, but he didn't wake. I thought he might be dead, but when I put a glass near his nose, it fogged up. There was no one else in the office, so I wrote a note to him and left.

I got home in three hours or so.

Several weeks later, I called to ask what he decided, if only out of curiosity. He told me that he was engaging someone else because he did not think I had enough industry experience. I asked him how he could come to that conclusion, since he was asleep for much of our discussion. No response!

FORENSIC WORK

I was retained by a law firm to do a forensic audit of a sausage company that was accused of adulterating their product. I asked what the adulterating was thought to be and was told they could not tell me. When I visited the company, I could not find anything obvious. I tested by taking the opening inventory in pounds; adding in purchases of ingredients; deducting sales in pounds, allowing for spoilage and shrinkage; and deducting the ending inventory. The sausage was "making babies"—there was too much.

I went to see the CFO and asked, "What kind of shit are you putting in the sausage?" He responded indignantly, "It is not shit. It is highly treated sewage effluent. You can eat it." Not me!

REAL-WORLD EXPERIENCE

I represented an agency owner in his divorce. The wife's valuation expert was a person who had written several books on valuation and was accepted as an expert by the judge. The opposing lawyer asked how many articles I had written. None. How many books or advanced degrees did I have? None.

When asked why I considered myself an expert in values of marketing services companies, I told the judge I had negotiated many sale transactions and was "in the room when checks were handed out." When he asked if I had read the books written by my opponent, I said I had tried but that they were not relevant and put me to sleep.

The judge asked the "expert" if he had ever participated in a real-world transaction in the business. "No," he replied. The judge then asked if he participated in a real-world transaction in any business. "No," he answered, "but I rely on publicly available information."

We then informed the judge that almost all transactions in this space were not reported publicly and that it was not possible to develop comparable transaction information. The expert admitted he could not locate any supporting information.

The parties settled that afternoon, out of court.

TROPHY WIFE

I saw a client in a restaurant across the room with a woman I did not recognize as his wife. I paid no attention to it and waved at him. He came over a bit later and asked if I wanted to meet his new trophy wife. I looked at her and said, "I guess you did not win first place."

SENATOR ALFONSE D'AMATO

I was at Senator Alfonse D'Amato's Park Strategies office on Park Avenue in New York. We were on a conference call with Mayor Ed Koch, Governor George Pataki, and several of Park Strategies' people. In the middle of the meeting, an assistant walked into the room and handed the senator a note. He immediately excused himself, asking everyone to stand by while he went to talk to his mother.

Quite touching!

XYZ PUBLIC RELATIONS

I was retained to do the tax and financial statement work for XYZ and later to sell the company.

When I looked at their records, I discovered that the profits were almost nonexistent. Their staff costs were high compared to their revenue. At an evening meeting in their offices, their CFO told me that they focused on overhead and not on people costs. I got up, turned out the lights in the room, and asked if their problems were eased. They got it, and with my help, within two years, they were profitable and costs were somewhat more under control.

They also assured me that their books were "clean" and that there were no personal or non-business-related costs. This was important for analytical, valuation, and tax reasons. The agency's costs also impact what clients' procurement people have submitted to them.

Much later, we learned that the unemployed brother-in-law, the gardener, the maid, and others were on the company's payroll.

The negotiated sale never did close.

KAREN SELLERS

Karen Sellers has worked with me for many years. When she had first started at my company, she was in a bind. She had bought a new house, but she was short $35,000. When she told me about her problem, I said I'd lend her the $35,000. She was shocked. She asked me what she needed to do for it. I told her, without hesitation, "Pay me back."

Up yours, Harvey Weinstein.

FRED GOLDBERG

Fred Goldberg was a senior person at Chiat/Day. When we met, he was running the San Francisco office. Jay "insisted" that Fred buy that office from Chiat/Day, and I was the negotiator opposite Fred.

Some years later, Fred retained me to sell his agency to the Lowe Group, part of Interpublic. I had told Fred the story of my Steuben lion shafting: one time, a client refused to pay me a transaction fee even though he acknowledged I did a great job; instead, he gave me a Steuben lion trophy, which cost about $3,000 versus the $100,000 he owed. In his style, after the closing, Fred sent me a box with a crystal ice bucket from Christofle. Buried in tissue paper was a very generous check and a note telling me to enjoy the bucket.

MARTIN PURIS

Martin Puris had quite a bit of Interpublic stock after its sale with a low income tax basis. I suggested he hedge or sell or do something to protect the value, as one should do in any concentrated position.

Martin called a contact of his who suggested we meet with a "Mr. Whit," as we will call him. We met, and after we explained the circumstances, he said he wanted to work on it and scheduled another discussion two weeks later. At that meeting, he rendered his advice—if Martin thought the stock was going up, hold it, but if he thought the stock was going down, sell it.

Dumbfounded, I asked why it took him two weeks to give us worthless advice. He had nothing to add, so we adjourned.

Some years later, Mr. Whit called me to tell me he was at another firm and asked if I'd like to meet. I told him I doubted he was smarter, so I passed.

JOHN WREN

After I hurt my leg one summer, I had to walk with a cane. I visited Omnicom for a meeting, and after it ended, the skies opened up and there was a tremendous thunderstorm. John Wren saw my face and asked where I was going. I told him I had to get to a ferry from Wall Street to make a doctor's appointment. He proceeded to walk me downstairs to his car and told his driver to take me where I needed to go. Wow!

SANDY KURTZIG

Sandy Kurtzig was the founder of a Silicon Valley firm. She was extremely intelligent and successful. Jay introduced us, and she eventually became a client.

One evening, I was reading some tax literature and saw something that would likely apply to her. I called her, and long story short, she saved over seven figures in income taxes. She paid me a fee but asked where I'd like to travel that I had never been to. I told her Hawaii!

Sandy arranged for Sheila and me to travel to Hawaii. We saw almost all the islands, stayed in the best hotels, ate in the finest restaurants, and traveled first class. Everything was paid for—I didn't even need to buy a newspaper. We spent several days with her and her fiancé and had a memorable time.

It made Sheila and I fans of Hawaii, and we have gone back annually for the last twenty-five years or so.

STUPID AND STUPIDER

I had a client send their pitch materials to DHL via FedEx.

I had a client's divisional CFO steal by submitting bills for meals and entertainment from a company called Builders General. Builders General is a lumberyard near my home. I asked him if he was entertaining termites.

I went on a trip to Wichita, Kansas, with a client's account management employee for a meeting. We expected to get home that same day, but I was told to bring a change of clothes and a toothbrush just in case. We missed the last flight home that evening, so we had to stay at a hotel. I went down in the morning to check both of us out and found out that his bill was hundreds of dollars more than mine. I wondered how many movies and how many minibar items he could have had. He had none, but he had brought his dirty laundry from home for the valet to wash.

I was visiting a client and friend of mine in order to play in a three-day golf tournament. I stayed at his condo and slept in the guest bedroom. The room had no bathroom, no phone, no intercom, thick walls, and a broken door that got stuck. When I woke up in the middle of the night with a full bladder, I was trapped.

I yelled, banged on the walls, yanked at the door, and tried to go back to sleep—nothing worked except my personal plumbing. I found a sealed can of collectable tennis balls and used it to relieve myself. My host was annoyed but admitted that the door had given him problems. When I showered that morning, the shower head fell off, and I washed in a small water stream. We did not win the golf tournament.

For my fortieth birthday in 1987, a client sent me a branded bottle of French wine from his personal cellar, vintage 1937. I opened the special bottle at a birthday dinner, and when I poured it, it was brown and smelled awful. We all got a great laugh.

That same client was invited to my daughter Laura's bat mitzvah. The ceremony was in the morning at our local temple and the reception was in the evening at a catering hall forty miles north. The client went to the temple in the evening in error, arrived at the reception three hours late, and complained to the band leader the music was too loud. The band-leader told him to give a big gift and he might get a better seat next time. He immediately left.

I had an architectural design client who wanted to sell her business. She had financial statements prepared by a well-regarded CPA firm that showed she was making substantial profits. She was also spending accordingly. During due diligence, the buyer discovered that the advance deposits the seller was collecting on projects from her clients were taken into income, so the income was overstated because there were no costs against the deposits. The accountant made no apologies and was fired when the business's growth slowed down, costs were incurred, and the cash-flow pressures and losses showed up.

During discussions to buy back an agency from a holding company, it became apparent that there was a disconnect between the two sides about the true profits being earned. The holding company believed the proposed buyer, my client, was lowballing. The holding company sent in their big CPA firm to check. Some weeks later at a meeting, the report was presented, and there was a large addition to profits proposed. As is typical, the agency incurred a material amount of new business costs, and some of the clients were not won. I calmly asked if there was any question the costs were incurred. None, I was told.

So why the additional addback? "Well," he said, "you did not win the business, so the cost to pitch the business was wasted."

My client's CFO held me back from jumping across the table at the pandering idiot who wrote the report. We made the deal soon thereafter.

There are tax-saving opportunities for New York City–based companies for sale. One major buyer disagreed with my position and mandated my client pay the unnecessary tax. We did and applied for a refund, which was received. The buyer claimed it was his, and an argument ensued over the large amount of money. We won.

That same opportunity presented itself when I was retained late in a sale process to assist with tax clauses. My client, the seller, had a large law firm working on the transaction. When I presented the idea one morning, the tax lawyer said the provision was repealed. I replied, "I went to bed early last night, so I might have missed the repeal, but I think it's in effect." I was correct, and he never surfaced again.

One time while a closing was going on, I was called at home at around two o'clock in the morning. My client, the seller, was freaked out about a legal issue raised by the lawyers on both sides. I washed my face and took the call—but I was not in a good mood.

I listened as the issue was explained. I asked each of the five lawyers on the phone how many years of experience they had. The aggregate was more than one hundred years. I asked if in that time, any of them had seen the issue, read a case on it, or heard of it being a concern. I got five immediate nos. We closed, and the issue has not come up in the last ten-plus years.

I represented a private equity firm that had invested in a marketing services company. The deal was not a success, and they wanted to sell. I received an offer for about 25 percent of the investment, but they refused it.

They asked if I thought I could get them their investment back if they offered me an incentive fee. I told them it was highly unlikely, but if I did, they'd have to pay for ass-wiping services for me for the rest of my life.

Less than a year later, they did happily sell for a very small sum.

I was retained by an ad agency to help them with their client's procurement people, who were asking for all kinds of financial information, such as cost, rent, payroll, overhead, profit margins, bonuses, standard hours, and so on. I did so and spent about eight hours on the project. The client saved about $600,000 per year and was aghast at my fees, which were less than $10,000. They told me I was too expensive and would not use me any further. Good!

I had a media-buying client that was paid in advance for the media and did not have enough cash to pay their payables. They were living on the float, which is very dangerous and wrong. In fact, the business was losing a great deal of money, as evidenced by the shortfall between their payables and their cash and receivables. The principals did not understand this, and we were asked to talk to their accountant, who prepared internal financials showing they were profitable.

We did talk to him, and he said he did the numbers off their books, effectively, on a cash basis and would give the numbers a "physic" at the end of the year. This meant he did nothing of value—a client payment was reported as income, and if they did not pay the media, there was no expense. Oh my!

I always give my wife a copy of my daily schedule if I am working away from home. One day I had a breakfast appointment with Buz Sawyer (who shared a name with an old comic strip) and a lunch appointment with Charlie Horsey—both real people with real names. Sheila called me and asked if I could not be more creative in my alleged agenda.

I had two clients who each had a mistress. They funded the mistresses' businesses, so I was involved and knew both of them. One of my client's sons married the other's daughter. A few months after the wedding, I was being seated at a restaurant for dinner and noticed a large table of six across the room. At the table were my two clients, their two mistresses, and the son/son-in-law and his mistress. I blushed and hustled to my table. I was called the next day and chastened for embarrassing them by not greeting them.

ANONYMOUS

There are others that I cannot identify by name in good conscience who lack a certain something.

One client was to receive a portion of the sales price in the buyer's stock. The buyer sent a stock certificate for ten times the correct number of shares, and he forbade me from telling the buyer of the error. As you'd imagine, the buyer soon discovered the error and asked me if I knew about it. Under instructions from my client and due to client confidentiality, all I could truthfully say was "No comment." Of course, once the error was discovered, the erroneous certificate was voided, and I was terminated by the client.

I had a client that called for a meeting with his lawyer and me. The meeting was to be from 10:30 a.m. until noon, and I billed the client for one and a half hours. The client called and told me that his lawyer billed for two and a half hours and asked me why. I was befuddled and called the lawyer, who explained he had to write a postmeeting memo. The client fired both the lawyer and me.

I had a longtime client whom I did tax work for. He sold his business to a British firm, who installed its own CFO. Some months later, I noticed that the former owners still had the business, now owned by a public company, pay for personal items. I asked them in private about those purchases, and they assured me that the CFO was aware of it. I told them I was obligated to verify it with him, and they reassured me it was agreed upon. I told the CFO, who thanked me for doing the right thing and told me he was, indeed, aware of it.

Three days later, I was fired by the CFO, who told me that the former owners lost confidence in me. He said he knew it was unfair, but he was sure it would be a good thing for me in the near future.

It was—Jay Chiat retained me a few days later.

I have been fortunate to represent many people whose talents are coupled with their humanity, reasonableness, fairness, and generosity of spirit. Being tough does not mean being mean or selfish. And I am happy to say that the overwhelming majority of people I have worked with and met during my career are people who are not lacking these traits that we all aspire to.

But there will always be some negative experiences along with the positives.

The Assets of

**Ming Utility and Entertainment Group LLC
and Affiliates**

have been acquired by
a wholly-owned subsidiary of

MDC Partners Inc.

We acted as strategic advisors to
the sellers and assisted in the negotiations.

DAVID C. WIENER AND COMPANY LLC
An Affiliate of EisnerAmper LLP

September, 2017

The Membership Interests of

**Love The 88 LLC
And Affiliates**

have been acquired by

Havas Creative, Inc.

We acted as strategic advisors to
the sellers and assisted in the negotiations.

DAVID WIENER AND COMPANY LLC
An Affiliate of EisnerAmper LLP

September, 2017

**GRAVITY MEDIA, LLC
and Affiliates**

have been acquired by

a wholly-owned subsidiary of

Dentsu Aegis Network

We acted as strategic advisors to
the sellers and assisted in negotiations

DAVID WIENER AND COMPANY LLC
An Affiliate of EisnerAmper LLP

November, 2016

A majority interest in

Go! Productions LLC

has been acquired from

a wholly owned subsidiary of

Omnicom Group Inc.

by

GOXD Holdings LLC.

We acted as finanical advisors to
the buyer and assisted in the negotiations.

David Wiener and Company LLC
An Affiliate of EisnerAmper LLP

November, 2016

The stock of
FORSMAN & BODENFORS AB
has been acquired by
a wholly owned subsidiary of
MDC Partners Inc.

---

*We acted as financial advisors to
the sellers and assisted in the negotiations.*

DAVID WIENER AND COMPANY LLC
AN AFFILIATE OF EISNERAMPER LLP

July 2016

Newco New Jersey LLC
has sold its assets to
Mercury Public Affairs LLC
a wholly-owned subsidiary of
Omnicom Group Inc.

---

*We acted as financial advisors
to the seller and assisted
in the negotiations.*

DAVID WIENER AND COMPANY LLC
AN AFFILIATE OF EISNERAMPER LLP

March 2015

Allison Brown Holdings, Inc.
has sold an additional minority interest in
Allison & Partners LLC
to a wholly-owned subsidiary of
MDC Partners Inc.

---

*We acted as strategic advisors
to the seller and assisted
in the negotiations.*

DAVID WIENER AND COMPANY LLC
AN AFFILIATE OF EISNERAMPER LLP

May 2015

David C. Wiener, CPA
Warren A. Suna, CPA
Harold Goldman, CPA
Carey C. Gertler, CPA

and

EisnerAmper LLP
have formed

DAVID WIENER AND COMPANY LLC
AN AFFILIATE OF EISNERAMPER LLP

November 2014

Alliant Holding I, L.P.
and its subsidiary
Alliant Insurance Services, Inc.
have acquired the operating assets of
ABC Benefits Consulting PA LLC

---

*We acted as advisors
to the seller and assisted
in the negotiations.*

DAVID WIENER AND COMPANY LLC
AN AFFILIATE OF EISNERAMPER LLP

December 2014

Alliant Insurance Services, Inc.
has acquired the stock of
Worth Corporate Planning, Inc.
and
American Benefits and Compensation Systems, Inc.

---

*We acted as advisors
to the seller and assisted
in the negotiations.*

DAVID WIENER AND COMPANY LLC
AN AFFILIATE OF EISNERAMPER LLP

December 2014

Shepardson Stern + Kaminsky LLC
has sold a minority interest to
M&C Saatchi Agency, Inc.
a wholly-owned subsidiary of
M&C Saatchi PLC

---

*We acted as strategic advisors
to the seller and assisted
in the negotiations.*

DAVID WIENER AND COMPANY LLC
AN AFFILIATE OF EISNERAMPER LLP

November 2014

A majority interest in

Hunter Public Relations, LLC

has been acquired by

a wholly owned subsidiary of

MDC Partners Inc.

We acted as financial advisors
to the seller and assisted in the negotiations.

DAVID C. WIENER AND COMPANY
A DIVISION OF COHNREZNICK LLP

August, 2014

MKTG, Inc.

has merged with

a wholly-owned subsidiary of

Aegis Lifestyle, Inc.

a wholly-owned subsidiary of

Dentsu Aegis Network

We acted as strategic advisors to
the seller and assisted in the negotiations.

DAVID C. WIENER
IN ASSOCIATION WITH
PALAZZO

August, 2014

Nunez LLC

has sold its assets to

Mercury Public Affairs LLC

a wholly owned subsidiary of

Omnicom Group Inc.

We acted as financial advisors
to the seller and assisted in the negotiations.

**DAVID C. WIENER AND COMPANY
A DIVISION OF COHNREZNICK LLP**

December, 2013

Michael Shine

has sold his stock to

BSS Advertising Inc.

an affiliate of

Butler, Shine, Stern & Partners LLC

We acted as financial advisors
to the seller and assisted in the negotiations.

**DAVID C. WIENER AND COMPANY
A DIVISION OF COHNREZNICK LLP**

January, 2014

The stock of

Paul Stuart, Inc.

has been acquired by

Mitsui & Co., Ltd.

We acted as financial advisors
to the sellers and assisted in the negotiations.

**DAVID C. WIENER AND COMPANY
A DIVISION OF COHNREZNICK LLP**

December, 2012

CAPSTRAT, Inc.

has sold its assets to

a wholly owned subsidiary of

Omnicom Group Inc.

We acted as financial advisors to
the seller and assisted in the negotiations.

**DAVID C. WIENER AND COMPANY
A DIVISION OF COHNREZNICK LLP**

December, 2012

An interest in

DONER PARTNERS LLC

has been acquired by
a wholly owned subsidiary of

MDC Partners Inc.

We acted as financial advisors
to the sellers and assisted in the negotiations.

**DAVID C. WIENER AND COMPANY
A DIVISION OF J.H. COHN LLP**

March, 2012

CHEIL USA INC.

has acquired 100%
of the membership interests in

McKinney Ventures LLC

d/b/a

McKinney

We acted as financial advisors
to the buyer and assisted in the negotiations.

**DAVID C. WIENER AND COMPANY
A DIVISION OF J.H. COHN LLP**

July, 2012

The stock of

Marina Maher Communications, Inc.

has been acquired by

DAS Group LLC

a wholly owned subsidiary of

Omnicom Group Inc.

We acted as financial advisors
to the seller and assisted in the negotiations.

**DAVID C. WIENER AND COMPANY
A DIVISION OF J.H. COHN LLP**

November, 2011

Cell Division, Inc.

has sold its assets to

EURO RSCG Healthview, Inc.

d/b/a

Havas Health Worldwide

We acted as financial advisors
to the seller and assisted in the negotiations.

**DAVID C. WIENER AND COMPANY
A DIVISION OF J.H. COHN LLP**

November, 2011

A majority interest in

Laird + Partners LLC

has been acquired by
a wholly owned subsidiary of

MDC Partners Inc.

We acted as financial advisors
to the seller and assisted in the negotiations.

**DAVID C. WIENER AND COMPANY
A DIVISION OF J.H. COHN LLP**

August, 2011

The stock of

Newmark & Company Real Estate, Inc.

and controlling interests in its affiliates

have been acquired by

BGC Partners, Inc.

We acted as tax advisors to the sellers.

**DAVID C. WIENER AND COMPANY
A DIVISION OF J.H. COHN LLP**

October, 2011

Fanscape, Inc.

has sold its assets to
a wholly owned subsidiary of

The Marketing Arm, Inc.

a wholly owned subsidiary of

Omnicom Group Inc.

We acted as financial advisors
to the seller and assisted in the negotiations.

**DAVID C. WIENER AND COMPANY
A DIVISION OF J.H. COHN LLP**

February, 2011

A majority interest in

72andSunny Partners LLC

has been acquired by
a wholly owned subsidiary of

MDC Partners Inc.

We acted as financial advisors
to the seller and assisted in the negotiations.

**DAVID C. WIENER AND COMPANY
A DIVISION OF J.H. COHN LLP**

December, 2010

A majority interest in

**RED Interactive Agency, LLC
and affiliates**

has been acquired by
a wholly owned subsidiary of

William Morris Endeavor Entertainment, LLC

We acted as financial advisors
to the buyer and assisted in the negotiations.

**DAVID C. WIENER AND COMPANY
A DIVISION OF J.H. COHN LLP**

August, 2010

An additional equity interest in

Go! Productions LLC

has been acquired by
a wholly owned subsidiary of

Omnicom Group Inc.

Go! Productions LLC

has merged with

C2 Creative LLC

to form

Go! LLC

We acted as financial advisors
to the seller and assisted in the negotiations.

**DAVID C. WIENER AND COMPANY
A DIVISION OF J.H. COHN LLP**

November, 2010

A majority interest in

**Team Enterprises, LLC
and affiliates**

has been acquired by
a wholly owned subsidiary of

MDC Partners Inc.

We acted as financial advisors
to the sellers and assisted in the negotiations.

**DAVID C. WIENER AND COMPANY
A DIVISION OF J.H. COHN LLP**

March, 2010

Epocrates, Inc.

has acquired the assets of

MedCafe, Inc.

and certain
intellectual property assets of

Seasons Media

We acted as financial advisors to
the buyer and assisted in the negotiations.

DAVID C. WIENER AND COMPANY
A DIVISION OF J.H. COHN LLP

February, 2010

The remaining equity interest in

PainePR LLC

has been acquired by
a wholly owned subsidiary of

Cossette Communication Group Inc.

We acted as financial advisors to
the sellers and assisted in the negotiations.

DAVID C. WIENER AND COMPANY
A DIVISION OF J.H. COHN LLP

January, 2009

The stock of

Express Finance (Bromley) Ltd.

has been acquired by

a wholly owned subsidiary of

Dollar Financial Corp.

We acted as advisors to the purchaser.

DAVID C. WIENER AND COMPANY
A DIVISION OF J.H. COHN LLP

April, 2009

A majority interest in

Paul Wilmot Communications LLC

has been acquired by

a wholly owned subsidiary of

Fleishman-Hillard Inc.

a wholly owned subsidiary of

Omnicom Group Inc.

We acted as financial advisors
to the seller and assisted in the negotiations.

DAVID C. WIENER AND COMPANY
A DIVISION OF J.H. COHN LLP

August, 2008

The remaining equity interest in

Endeavor Marketing, LLC

has been acquired by

The Interpublic Group of Companies, Inc.

from a wholly-owned limited liability company of

Mark Dowley and Endeavor Agency, LLC

We acted as financial advisors to
the sellers and assisted in the negotiations.

**DAVID C. WIENER AND COMPANY
A DIVISION OF J.H. COHN LLP**

March, 2008

United Entertainment Group
(A Delaware Limited Liability Company)

has been formed by

Jarrod Moses

and

United Talent Agency, Inc.

We acted as financial advisors to
Mr. Moses and assisted in the negotiations.

**DAVID C. WIENER AND COMPANY
A DIVISION OF J.H. COHN LLP**

September, 2007

The remaining equity interest in

Mercury Public Affairs, LLC

has been acquired by

a wholly owned subsidiary of

Omnicom Group Inc.

We acted as financial advisors
to the sellers and assisted in the negotiations.

**DAVID C. WIENER AND COMPANY
A DIVISION OF J.H. COHN LLP**

March, 2008

Colangelo Synergy Marketing, Inc.

has sold its assets to

a wholly owned subsidiary of

Omnicom Group Inc.

We acted as finanical advisors to
the seller and assisted in the negotiations.

**DAVID C. WIENER AND COMPANY
A DIVISION OF J.H. COHN LLP**

Autumn, 2006

A majority interest in

The Leverage Group, Inc.

has been acquired by

MEDIAEDGE:cia, LLC

a wholly owned subsidiary of

WPP Group plc

We acted as finanical advisors to
the seller and assisted in the negotiations.

DAVID C. WIENER AND COMPANY
A DIVISION OF J.H. COHN LLP

March, 2006

A majority interest in

**Kirshenbaum Bond & Partners LLC
and affiliates**

has been acquired by

a wholly owned subsidiary of

MDC Partners Inc.

We acted as financial advisors
to the sellers and assisted in the negotiations.

DAVID C. WIENER AND COMPANY
A DIVISION OF J.H. COHN LLP

January, 2004

A majority interest in

PainePR LLC

has been acquired by

a wholly owned subsidiary of

Cossette Communication Group Inc.

We acted as finanical advisors to
the sellers and assisted in the negotiations.

DAVID C. WIENER AND COMPANY
A DIVISION OF J.H. COHN LLP

October, 2004

A majority interest in

Mercury Public Affairs, LLC

has been acquired by

a wholly owned subsidiary of

Omnicom Group Inc.

We acted as finanical advisors to
the sellers and assisted in the negotiations.

DAVID C. WIENER AND COMPANY
A DIVISION OF J.H. COHN LLP

October, 2003

Pierce Promotions and Event Management, Inc.

has sold its assets to

a wholly owned subsidiary of

Omnicom Group Inc.

We acted as financial advisors to
the seller and assisted in the negotiations.

DAVID C. WIENER AND COMPANY
A DIVISION OF J.H. COHN LLP

June, 2003

C2 Creative, Inc.

has sold its assets to

a wholly-owned subsidiary of

Omnicom Group Inc.

We acted as financial advisors to
the seller and assisted in the negotiations.

DAVID C. WIENER AND COMPANY
A DIVISION OF J.H. COHN LLP

December, 2001

Siegelgale, Inc.

has sold its assets to

a wholly-owned subsidiary of

Omnicom Group Inc.

We acted as finanical advisors
to the seller and assisted
in the negotiations.

DAVID WIENER AND COMPANY LLC
A DIVISION OF J.H. COHN LLP

May, 2003

DeVries Public Relations, Ltd.

has sold its assets to

a wholly-owned subsidiary of

The Interpublic Group of Companies, Inc.

We acted as financial advisors to
the seller and assisted in the negotiations.

DAVID C. WIENER AND COMPANY
A DIVISION OF J.H. COHN LLP

August, 2001

Post & Partners Inc.

has been sold to

Cossette Communication Group Inc.

We acted as finanical advisors to
the seller and assisted in the negotiations.

**DAVID C. WIENER AND COMPANY LLC
A DIVISION OF J.H. COHN LLP**

August, 2001

A Minority Equity Interest in

Crispin Porter & Bogusky LLC

has been acquired by
a wholly owned subsidiary of

Maxxcom Inc.

a subsidiary of

MDC Corporation Inc.

We acted as financial advisors to
the seller and assisted in the negotiations.

DAVID C. WIENER AND COMPANY
A DIVISION OF J.H. COHN LLP

January 2001

The stock of

Deutsch, Inc.

has been purchased by

a wholly-owned subsidiary of

The Interpublic Group of Companies, Inc.

We acted as financial and tax advisors to
the sellers and assisted in the negotiations.

DAVID C. WIENER AND COMPANY
A DIVISION OF J.H. COHN LLP

November, 2000

The stock of

Zimmerman & Partners Advertising, Inc.

has been sold to

Zimmerman Holdings Group Inc.

a wholly owned subsidiary of

Omnicom Group Inc.

We acted as financial advisors to
the sellers and assisted in the negotiations.

DAVID C. WIENER AND COMPANY
A DIVISION OF J.H. COHN LLP

April, 1999

The stock of

DFG Holdings, Inc.

has been acquired by

Members of Management

and

Green Equity Investors II, L.P.

an affiliate of

Leonard Green & Partners, L.P.

We acted as financial and tax advisors to
management and assisted in the negotiations.

DAVID C. WIENER AND COMPANY
A DIVISION OF J.H. COHN LLP

December, 1998

The assets of

MICHAEL KOOPER ENTERPRISES INC.
d/b/a
THE KOOPER GROUP

have been acquired by

TKG ACQUISITION CORP.
a wholly owned subsidiary of
LOWNDES LAMBERT US HOLDINGS INC.
and
LAMBERT FENCHURCH GROUP PLC

We acted as financial and tax advisors to
the sellers and assisted in the negotiations.

DAVID C. WIENER AND COMPANY
A DIVISION OF J.H. COHN LLP

November, 1997

The stock of

Carmichael Lynch, Inc.

has been purchased by

The Interpublic Group of Companies

We acted as finanical advisors to
the sellers and assisted in the negotiations.

DAVID C. WIENER AND COMPANY
A DIVISION OF J.H. COHN LLP

April, 1998

David C. Wiener and Company
A Professional Corporation
Certified Public Accountants

has sold its assets to

J.H. COHN LLP
ACCOUNTANTS & CONSULTANTS

The firm will conduct its
accounting and consulting practice as

DAVID C. WIENER AND COMPANY
A DIVISION OF J.H. COHN LLP

May, 1997

Chiat/Day Holdings, Inc.

and

Chiat/Day inc. Advertising

have sold their assets to

TBWA International Inc.

a wholly owned subsidiary of

Omnicom Group Inc.

We acted as financial and tax advisors to the sellers
in the transactions and assisted in the negotiations

David C. Wiener and Company

August, 1995

The majority interest in

Fallon McElligott, Inc.

has been acquired from

Scali, McCabe, Sloves, Inc.

a subsidiary of

WPP Group, Inc.

by an investment group formed by
the minority owners and other members of management.

We acted as financial advisor to the Buyers
in this transaction and assisted in the negotiations.

David C. Wiener and Company

October, 1993

The assets of

Campbell Mithun Esty, Inc.

(A Subsidiary of Cordiant PLC)

have been acquired by
a limited liability company formed by
members of management

and

The Interpublic Group of Companies

We acted as financial advisor to the Buyers
in this transaction and assisted in the negotiations

David C. Wiener and Company

April, 1995

The Principals of

Goodby, Berlin & Silverstein, Inc.

have sold their majority interest to

a wholly owned subsidiary of

Omnicom Group Inc.

We acted as financial advisor to the principals of
Goodby, Berlin & Silverstein, Inc. in this transaction
and assisted in the negotiations.

David C. Wiener and Company

January, 1992

ABOUT THE AUTHOR

David and Sheila Wiener, 2018

David C. Wiener is the founder and a member of David Wiener and Company LLC, an affiliate of EisnerAmper LLP. With more than forty-five years of public accounting experience, David's practice focuses on advertising agencies and other marketing communications companies. He serves these firms with a range of accounting and consulting expertise that includes merger and acquisition advisory services, finance and business development, tax and estate planning, business negotiations, executive compensation, litigation settlements, and other management advisory services.

With more than three hundred marketing communications companies composing his past and current client base, David has represented many well-known names in the industry, such as Deutsch; Goodby, Silverstein & Partners; Kirshenbaum & Bond; Fallon; Mercury Public Affairs; Ammirati & Puris; 72andSunny; Crispin Porter + Bogusky; William Morris Endeavor; Doner; Gravity Media; Carmichael Lynch; Forsman & Bodenfors; and Marina Maher Communications. Prior to the purchase by Omnicom, David represented and was a director of Chiat/Day inc. Advertising.

SMITH PUBLICITY, INC.
FOR REVIEW ONLY
RESALE PROHIBITED
Excluding Nonprofit Organizations